VIA FOLIOS 64

Profiles of Italian Americans

MARIE,

KEEP UP THE GOOD WORK

PRESERVING OUR ITALIAN

AMERICAN HERITAGE.

Cosmo Ferrara

Profiles of

ITALIAN AMERICANS

Achieving the Dream
and
Giving Back

Cosmo F. Ferrara, Ed.D.

BORDIGHERA PRESS

Library of Congress Control Number: 2010906732

ϸ /6.⁰⁰ 28 CHRIS AVE-
HILLSDALE, NJ 07642

Printed in the United States.

Published by
BORDIGHERA PRESS
John D. Calandra Italian American Institute
25 W. 43rd Street, 17th Floor
New York, NY 10036

VIA FOLIOS 64
ISBN 978–1–59954–016–0

To Frances, Always

Contents

To the Reader

There are between 17 million and 25 million Italian Americans living in the United States, depending on the statistical data you use. According to the US Census 2000, Italian Americans comprise the country's fifth largest ethnic group. Yet the only image that many people have of Italian Americans is the one they see on television and in the movies. And that image of gangsters, bimbos, and buffoons is an outrageous distortion.

The large majority of Italian Americans are law-abiding, hard-working citizens who raise families, engender strong values, and contribute to the overall well-being of their communities and the country. Yet this image is overshadowed by the negative Hollywood stereotypes.

The Book's Purpose

The purpose of this book is to counter the negative stereotypes and to put Italian Americans in the proper perspective. The book profiles 32 Italian Americans in action, achieving the American dream and fulfilling that dream by giving back to society. These 32 women and men represent, through their work and commitment to others, millions of their unnamed and unheralded counterparts.

Many Italian Americans know too little about their heritage and, as a result, do not take pride it. Through these profiles, this book shows why they have every right to be proud.

The Profiles

Profiled here are men and women who have achieved success in a wide range of careers: business, public service, the military, law enforcement, medicine, research, the arts, journalism, science, sports, education, the media, and humanitarian activities. The criteria for inclusion in this group are these:

1. *The person is Italian American.* Italians such as Michaelangelo and DaVinci are universally respected, so there is no need to acknowledge their contributions here. Our focus is on Italian Americans.

2. *The person has achieved success*—realized the American Dream, if you will.
3. *The person has enriched the lives of others,* in the true spirit of America.
4. *The person's story makes an interesting read.*

Whether or not you have Italian blood coursing through your veins, you may have heard of some of the people profiled in the book, but do not know the details of their lives. For instance, you may know of Peter Rodino, who presided over the Watergate hearings with such dignity he restored confidence in the American political and justice systems. You may have heard of Mother Francis Xavier Cabrini, who founded hospitals, schools, and orphanages for countless thousands.

You may be less familiar with Angela Bambace, who led the fight for better working conditions in the garment industry after the tragic Triangle Shirtwaist fire, and Edmund D. Pellegrino, MD, who overcame ethnic prejudice to eventually become Chair of the President's Council on Bioethics.

Gaining a Greater Sense of Pride

Reading of these men and women will wipe away the feeling that we need to take a defensive stance as Italian Americans. Instead, reading these profiles should inspire Italian Americans of every generation to stand tall and speak with pride of their great heritage and the contributions that Italian Americans have made—and continue to make—to help build a strong America.

Cosmo F. Ferrara, Ed.D.
Hillsdale, NJ
July 2009

ACKNOWLEDGEMENTS

I want to thank a number of people for their help in developing and publishing *Profiles of Italian Americans: Achieving the Dream and Giving Back*.

Among these are my family—immediate and extended—for their encouragement and enthusiasm for the project. In particular, I single out my wife, Frances, who read the manuscript for every profile—often more than once—and gave me her honest opinions but did so with the utmost tact and sensitivity.

I also thank Ralph La Rossa for his constant support and my friends at IHA for their unconditional acceptance.

My thanks go to Marion and A.J. "Buddy" Fortunato of *The Italian Tribune* who suggested candidates for inclusion and gathered some research information. I also thank Paul Basile and members of the staff at *Fra Noi* who went well beyond expectations, even contributing copy.

I am grateful to the people at the John D. Calandra Italian American Institute, Queens College, CUNY, particularly Anthony Tamburri and Fred Gardaphe, as well as Paolo Giordano, for their confidence in my material and their offer to publish it as a book with Bordighera Press. To Lisa Cicchetti, who brought my material to the attention of the Institute and designed the cover, I say a special "thank you."

Finally, I thank the members of UNICO National whose motto "Service above Self" is the epitome of every person profiled in this book, and the Coccia Foundation, particularly Joseph Coccia, whose continuous efforts to promote the Italian American heritage were a driving force behind my desire to write this book.

I want to acknowledge those individuals and organizations that granted me permission to use material—photos and/or substantial text—from other works. These sources include: John Wiley & Sons, (Fiorello LaGuardia); Paul Basile and *Fra Noi* (Gil Mazzolin, Amy Mazzolin, Anthony Fornelli, and Renato Turano); Frederick T. Courtright, The Permissions

Company (John Ciardi); Marion Fortunato (Armando Alagna); Fr. Pierre Celestine Ndong, St. Isidore Church, (Mother Frances Cabrini); Mentoring USA (Matilda Cuomo); *Catholic Herald* (Father Vincent Capodanno); NIAF, Elissa Ruffino (Marie Garibaldi); Penn State University Department of Public Information (Joseph Paterno); Rick Spencer, Obici Healthcare Foundation (Amadeo Obici).

I am especially grateful to the following people who gave me personal photographs, hours of interview time, and insights into their lives so I could develop their profiles accurately though briefly: Betty DellaCorte, Matilda Cuomo, Frank Musorrafiti, Marylou Tibaldo-Bongiorno, and Jerome Bongiorno.

PROFILES

Amadeo Peter "A.P." Giannini
Banker

On April 18, 1906, an earthquake brought the
city of San Francisco to its knees. Buildings collapsed,
roadways ruptured, and fires raged up one street and
down another. Amid the resulting chaos, some saw this
as an opportunity, and looters were out scavenging all
they could carry. Amadeo Peter "A.P." Giannini sized up
the situation quickly. He borrowed a horse-drawn
wagon filled with produce and maneuvered his way
through the crumbling city to his bank, the Bank of

Italy. He dug through the rubble and was able to pile $2 million in gold, coins,
and securities onto the wagon, covering it with the produce to keep it out of
hands of the looters.[1]

With his depositors' savings secure, he quickly took the next step.
Though most banks wanted to remain closed until some sense of normalcy
returned to the city, Giannini set up temporary quarters on the docks near
San Francisco's North Beach. Using a plank laid across two barrels as a desk,
he issued credit on the strength of a face, a pledge, and a handshake, to help
customers rebuild their homes and their businesses. Many cite Giannini's re-
sourcefulness and quick action as a major factor in San Francisco's recovery.

From Produce to Banking

A first-generation Italian American, Amadeo Peter "A.P." Giannini was
born in 1870 in San Jose, California. Both his parents had immigrated to
the United States from Liguria, near Genoa, Italy. When Giannini was seven
years old, his father, a farmer, was killed, reportedly during an argument
over a dollar. His mother later remarried a produce merchant who took to
young Giannini and taught him the produce business. When Giannini was

---

[1]Daniel Kadlec, "Amadeo Peter Giannini. Builders & Titans. The Time 100," 12/7/98.
http://www.time.com/time/time100/builders/profile/giannini.html

18

14, he dropped out of school and worked full time with his stepfather. Showing industriousness, alertness, and good people skills, Giannini became a partner in the business after a few years. At 31, he sold his share of the business and planned to "retire." Those plans were short lived, however, when he accepted an appointment as a director of the Columbus Savings & Loan Association.

There he soon found himself in conflict with other directors, primarily over his desire to serve working class people. Until that time, banks accepted deposits from and made loans to only wealthy individuals and businesses, those who had money and collateral. From his work with farmers, merchants, and others, Giannini knew entire groups of people could not open savings accounts or get loans from banks, hard-working people who would indeed be good risks. Giannini insisted that expanding the customer base to working class families and small businesses would lead to the bank's growth. When the other directors refused to budge, he left Columbus S&L. With $150,000 he borrowed from his stepfather and 10 other investors, he opened his own bank, the Bank of Italy, in a former saloon directly across the street from Columbus S&L. He kept the bartender on as an assistant teller.[2]

Helping the Little People

Giannini knew that many poor people, especially of Italian backgrounds, would not enter a bank to ask for a loan. So Giannini went door-to-door and approached people on the street.[3] He quickly grew a roster of customers—mostly "little people"—and a sizable number of deposits. In addition to opening the banking process to the non-wealthy, many of whom were immigrants from a variety of countries in addition to Italy, Giannini introduced a number of other new banking practices. He extended banking hours, so customers could do their banking after finishing their work. He offered home mortgages and home equity loans, and, later, auto loans. He made credit respectable and reasonable—all while seeing the bank turn a profit.

---

[2]Kadlec. http://www.time.com/time/time100/builders/profile/giannini.html
[3]Mike Brewster. "A.P. Giannini: A Farsighted Banker," BusinessWeek Online, June 8, 2004. http://www.businessweek.com/bwdaily/dnflash/jun2004/nf2004068_1653_db078.htm

Taking a Risk

Besides taking a chance on the "little people," Giannini also accepted other "risky" customers. He made loans to vineyards, helping the wine industry get its start. His bank made a hefty loan to movie stars Charlie Chaplin and Mary Pickford when they wanted to create United Artists Studios. When Walt Disney ran over budget in filming *Snow White,* Giannini approved a $2 million loan. When the construction of the Golden Gate Bridge was delayed 14 years because of lack of funding, Giannini's bank bought six million dollars worth of bonds to launch the project.[4]

During the Great Depression of the 1930s, as runs on banks caused many to collapse, Giannini convinced many depositors to keep their money in the banks where it could work for them and help revive the economy, he said. He was again successful and his actions in this endeavor were said to be the inspiration in part for the character George Bailey in Frank Capra's movie classic *It's a Wonderful Life.*

Bank of America

Giannini's experience during the earthquake had taught him two points that stayed with him throughout his career. The first is the importance of having sufficient gold and hard cash on hand to meet any demand, even one driven by catastrophe or panic. And second, big banks are less vulnerable to crises and regional downturns than small banks are. It was this second point that drove him to expand across California and then across America as regulations would allow. He bought one small bank after another, adding branches to the Bank of Italy. The big move came in 1929 when he joined with Bank of America in New York and adopted that name.[5]

But the initial merger between the Bank of Italy and Bank of America was not without its problems. The New York banking establishment did not take easily this upstart bank's moving into its turf. Some tried belittling

---

[4]People and Events: Amadeo Peter Giannini (1870–1949).
http://www.pbs.org/wgbh/amex/goldengate/peopleevents/p_giannini.html
[5]Brewster.
http://www.businessweek.com/bwdaily/dnflash/jun2004/nf2004068_1653_db078.htm

Giannini with epithets like "Sicilian fruit merchant."[6] But Giannini withstood all challenges and the merger came off.

Years later, in 2004, some 50-plus years after Giannini's death, Bank of America completed a $48 billion purchase of FleetBoston Financial. One commentator, Ron Chernow, said the purchase "fulfills a vision that A.P. Giannini . . . articulated in 1904. It's taken the entire century to reach a truly national banking system."[7] One can easily imagine what Giannini's reaction would be to the banking crisis of 2008.

The Money Itch

Giannini died in 1949 at the age of 79. At the time, Bank of America had become the largest bank in the world, with assets of $7 billion and 526 branches in more than 300 United States cities.[8] At his death, Giannini's estate was about $500,000, a small amount for a man of his stature and success. That was because he did not want to acquire great wealth. He feared it might cause him to lose contact with the "little people" who meant so much to his success. For years he accepted virtually no pay, and when he was given a $1.5 million grant, he gave it all to the University of California. "Money itch is a bad thing," he said. "I never had that trouble."[9]

Honors, Awards, and Recognition
- A middle school in San Francisco is named after Giannini.
- The U.S. Postal Service recognized Giannini's contributions to American banking by issuing a postage stamp bearing his portrait in 1973.
- *TIME Magazine* named Giannini one of the 100 "builders and titans" of the twentieth century. He was the only banker included in that group.

---

[6] Brewster.
http://www.businessweek.com/bwdaily/dnflash/jun2004/nf2004068_1653_db078.htm
[7] "Marrying Money," The News Hour with Jim Lehrer Transcript, online Focus.
http://www.pbs.org/newshour/bb/business/jan-june98/mergers_4-13.html
[8] Brewster.
http://www.businessweek.com/bwdaily/dnflash/jun2004/nf2004068_1653_db078.htm
[9] Kadlec. http://www.time.com/time/time100/builders/profile/giannini.html

- *American Banker Magazine* recognized Giannini as one of the five most influential bankers of the twentieth century.
- As part of its 75th anniversary in 2004, *BusinessWeek* named Giannini one of the top 75 Great Innovators of the previous 75 years.
- The A.P. Giannini Foundation supports medical research fellowships and organizations engaged in research to improve the quality of life for people with hemophilia. The foundation has awarded some $12 million in support of 550 fellowships.[10]

---

[10]Frequently Asked Questions: http://www.apgianninifoundation.org/faq.html
Photo: http://www.apgianinni.com

BETTY DELLACORTE
Humanitarian

"'Where's my gun? Where did you hide it? Trying to put something over on me again. Where the hell did you hide it?'

Patty, my husband, was drunk and dissipated. He searched through the furniture in the room. I had hidden his gun and he knew it. He kept searching, tearing apart every drawer in the dresser. I was too terrified to speak. I tried not to tremble. I hoped that not reacting to him would prevent whatever action he had in mind. Surprisingly, he turned abruptly as if something or someone called to him and walked slowly out of the room. I hoped that was the end of it. My heart was beating fast. Was that the end of it? Had he given up and left the house? After a while I started to breathe easily again, and the cool breeze lulled me back to sleep.

"Suddenly, what seemed like hours later, the bedroom door burst open, and without warning Patty leaped upon me, his knees folded under his over-6-foot frame, pressing his crushing weight against my chest. I could barely breathe. Fury and hate-filled wildness blazed within his green, bloodshot eyes. His right hand held the butt of the gun like a club, as he slammed it repeatedly against the side of my head, cursing when he missed as I twisted from side to side.

"I could not move or cry out, 'Oh my God, is this a nightmare? Where did he find the gun?'

"My eyes clamped shut, more so I could not see his frightening, insane glare than to watch the gun descend. He rained more curses and blows upon my stunned body and head. 'This time I'm going to blow your head off.'

"There was nothing more I could do."

Betty DellaCorte, *Storm Within the Shelter*[1]

---

[1]Betty DellaCorte, *Shelter from the Storm* (Glendale, AZ: Villa Press, 1985 and Glendale, AZ: Elan Press, 2002). Information here came from interviews with Betty DellaCorte. photo: *Storm Within the Shelter* (Glendale, AZ: Elan Press, 2002).

Betty DellaCorte was born into a large Italian American family in Brooklyn, New York, in April, 1933. Her father was born in Italy; her mother, of Italian parents, in the United States. With many aunts, uncles, and cousins living nearby, Betty enjoyed many a family gathering. She recalls her father's joy of singing—and his love of wine. Betty also remembers that on many occasions he would yell at her mother for some fabricated reason. The yelling and shouting would become so loud that Betty and her sister, Flo, would hide. "Why doesn't Mom answer him back?" Betty thought as she cringed behind a bathroom door. She resented her mother's "weakness" for not standing up for herself, or for them.

In the name of "discipline," their very strict father often used his heavy hand on his daughters. Betty grew up feeling that "Nothing I did was ever right at home." In their teenage years, the girls were terrified if their father found out they had been out with boys. In later years, after marriage, Betty's parents became less rigid and more supportive of their daughters and grandchildren.

Her First Marriage

At the age of 18, Betty met Andre, who was seven years older than she, and a scholar. Because of his intellect and coming from an Italian family, Andre won over Betty's parents. Although Betty was reluctant, the two were married soon after. Betty later said that though the "magic" between herself and Andre was never there for her, she thought she "could learn to love him." Andre turned out to be an inattentive, unresponsive husband. Feeling trapped, Betty, at one time tried to solve her dilemma with sleeping pills, which only made matters worse. The couple had three children—two daughters and a son, the latter dying in infancy. Andre had many fears, especially taking any responsibility for his daughters when they were toddlers. Betty poured all the love she had into the two girls, Robin and Lisa.

Over the years, Andre's inattentiveness turned to yelling and screaming. Ironically, neighbors would ask: "Why don't you answer or yell back at him?" Betty's words as a young girl regarding her mother's acquiescence were echoing back to haunt her because she had no answer. Andre's business had them move to Ohio, where Betty sought the advice of professionals. She knew, and Andre knew, that 11 years of a loveless, dysfunctional marriage were over.

From Bad to Worse

Betty and her daughters moved to Arizona, following Betty's sister and her family. Betty took a position as a decorator for Montgomery Ward, where she met Patty Ryan, an Irishman who was quite a charmer and a drinker. After dating awhile, Patty encouraged Betty to leave Ward's to accept the offer to become an interior decorator for a more prestigious design company. Things were looking up.

Only after she married Patty did she learn that he had been married four times prior. He was the father of a number of children, though he doubted some of those were actually his, as all of his wives, he contended, "cheated" on him. He had a violent streak, which Betty saw a number of times, including once when he struck out against his own mother. He often accused Betty of dating other guys. He wanted her to leave the group of men with whom she was working.

The marriage was fraught with Patty's accusations, yelling, and eventual beatings. Betty made many calls to the police, who at times sided with Patty that his wife was making things up. Betty often filed charges, then dropped them. She initiated legal separations, then, after Patty again promised "to never do it again," she would change her mind. At each attempt to break away, Betty saw herself at fault, feeling that she instigated the trouble and set Patty off. And besides that, the girls seemed to adore him and he was good to them. She was the disciplinarian in the house and he was always the "good guy."

Hitting Bottom

To avoid having to make excuses for her facial bruises and her absences at the companies she worked for, again with Patty's encouragement, Betty quit her job and began her own interior decorating business, remodeling her garage into a design studio. As Robin and Lisa grew older and started to have minds of their own, they began to challenge Patty, realizing he was no longer their "hero." In Betty's absence, he turned on her older daughter, Robin, and her friends, terrifying them. Betty knew she had to get the strength to "escape."

She began attending Al-Anon meetings for the families of alcoholics. Following Al-Anon's 12-step program, she did become stronger. She no longer tried to manipulate Patty, but learned better ways of keeping herself and her children safe. Perhaps most importantly, she began to regain her own sense of self-worth. Eventually she took back her power and filed for divorce, and went through with it.

Rainbow Retreat: The First Shelter in the Nation for Battered Women

One night a woman Betty had met at an Al-Anon meeting showed up on Betty's doorstep. Her husband had locked her and her four children out. Betty took them in, and the idea for Rainbow Retreat was conceived. This became the first known shelter for battered women in the United States. There had been "Safe Homes" in which families volunteered a room for the night, but never one that specifically housed the victims of abuse in a therapeutic setting.

With a few like-minded women, Betty and her friend Joanne Rhoads, rented a house, cleaned, repaired, and furnished it. Not long after, the house became a refuge for a steady stream of women and children, all desperately seeking a roof for a short period of time, and some relief from their abusive spouses. The name Rainbow Retreat came to Betty from a poem she read about Niagara Falls, describing a calm river flowing slowly until it reaches a precipice. It falls hundreds of feet and is broken and shattered by the rocks below. Out of this turbulence and violence, however, rises a beautiful rainbow. "How true this was with us," Betty recalled. "Out of utter chaos in our lives, sometimes something beautiful happens."

Betty and her colleagues at Rainbow Retreat, through the 12-step program, did bring comfort, strength, and hope into the lives of dozens and eventually hundreds of battered women and children. Though a woman's stay at the house was limited, usually to 30 days, many were able to strengthen themselves. Some were able to find jobs that brought them self-respect and an income. In some instances, the husbands, knowing that their wives were seeking help, sought help for themselves. Eventually, together, some rebuilt their marriages.

Faith House

In 1972, building on the success of Rainbow Retreat, Betty transformed her own home into a second shelter on the west side of Phoenix, in Glendale. She called the shelter Faith House. Betty would not seek funding from government agencies, as was done for Rainbow Retreat. Nor would Faith House solicit donations. Betty had faith in a Higher Power that would somehow bring to this fledgling enterprise whatever was needed. And that is what happened. People heard about the work Faith House was doing, and offered legal and other professional services, goods, food, and money needed to help rebuild lives. This was a house of many miracles.

Serving Thousands in Need

Aside from the many challenges they faced in organizing, operating, and maintaining these shelters, Betty and her team had to deal with women of all types and dispositions. They tried to counsel and encourage women who suffered abuse that was no less than horrid, even bestial. They had to contend with belligerent husbands who would demand to see their wives. They also had to mollify neighbors fearful of what might happen to their neighborhood.

Over a period of years, Faith House became an agency that provided a range of services related to domestic violence in all its forms. Besides the shelters for abused women and children, Betty developed outpatient services and treatment for offenders, managed by her younger daughter, Lisa. Faith House also spawned The Valley Youth Organization, sponsoring in-school programs for children. In 1980, Faith House opened an additional home in Prescott, Arizona, under the direction of her older daughter, Robin.

Making People Aware

Perhaps most significantly, Betty raised the level of awareness of domestic violence and its effects. New laws have been passed in most states authorizing police to restrain and arrest the batterer without having a police officer personally witness the violence, as had been required previously. Twelve years after Betty opened Rainbow Retreat and Faith House, there were 16 other shelters in Arizona and 800 across the country. In that year, police responded to some 25,000 domestic violence calls in Phoenix alone—an average of 68 a day.

By 1990, Betty's 17th year of involvement in domestic violence, Faith House Agencies had sheltered more than 11,000 residents and helped 12,000 outpatient offenders. By the year 2000, The Faith House Agencies had helped over 30,000 individuals affected by domestic abuse and victimization. Today, there are thousands of shelters for victims of domestic violence across the country following the lead of Betty DellaCorte. Women know they do not have to live in fear of domestic violence.

Postscript

Betty had always been a hands-on manager of Faith House. But as it grew, a Board was appointed to oversee its operations. Betty still ran things. She also raised $3.5 million to build her final dream home that would house 75 women and their children. This facility would be built on a peaceful five acres of land that had a park-like setting, filled with trees and grass. It would have job training. Women and their children could live there for a year.

After her project was completed, new Corporate Board members believed that Faith House could no longer be run like a Mom and Pop operation. That meant, with Betty as the leader. Against Betty's wishes, the Board merged Faith House with a large corporate organization for the homeless. It summarily stripped Betty of her duties and directed her to clear out her office. She had become a pawn in a political battle for control of Faith House. The Founder, the Matriarch, was being shoved out the door.

"It was a nightmare I never saw coming," Betty said. She was filled with feelings of betrayal and loss, "as if they were taking my child from my arms and stabbing it right in front of me." Fortunately, daughter Robin had the foresight to ask Betty to cut the Prescott Faith House free before this *coup d'etat* took place. She did, and that house, now called "Stepping Stones," continues to grow under Robin's direction, assisted by Robin's daughter, Cori.

Rather than enter into a prolonged and expensive legal battle, Betty took the advice of her lawyer and accepted the Board's settlement offer. "I was a victim of another pervasive but often ignored form of abuse. It was not the abuse of alcohol but of corporate politics and greed."

Though they took away her creation, no one could ever take away the great feeling she enjoys knowing she had been there for thousands of victims in need. And as her friends wrote about her: "Despite the full circle she has taken, her dedication, commitment and faith help her triumph as a survivor."

FIORELLO H. LA GUARDIA
Congressman, Mayor

One cold winter night in 1932, when Fiorello
H. La Guardia was a US Congressman, a man from
his district walked into his New York office com-
plaining that the gas had been turned off in his
apartment and that his children were cold. After
finding out that the gas had been turned off with-
out any prior notice from the company, La
Guardia called the governor's office, although it
was late, and secured the home phone number of
the public service commissioner. He blasted the
commissioner and the gas company, and warned that he would begin inves-
tigations in Congress unless something was done to help this unfortunate
man and his family. The gas company sent out an emergency crew, which
quickly restored heat to the man's apartment.[1]

Standing barely five-foot-two, stocky, and often wearing a Stetson cow-
boy hat and western string bow tie, La Guardia spoke in a high-pitched
squeaky voice. He spoke Yiddish to Jews, German to Germans, Croatian to
Croats, Hungarian to Hungarians, Italian to Italians, and English to anyone
else who would listen.[2] Always flamboyant, he had a flair for the dramatic.
As Mayor of New York, he went on radio and read the comics to the children
during a newspaper strike. He donned a firefighter's hat, slicker, and boots
and coordinated efforts at major fires and disasters. In his war against illegal
gambling, he had dozens of slot machines confiscated and piled high and
then he slammed them with a sledge hammer. These actions were taken with
political implications in mind, to be sure, but they were also done to stress

[1]Ronald H. Bayor, *Fiorello La Guardia: Ethnicity and Reform* (Wheeling, IL: Harlan David-
son, 1993) 76.
[2]H. Paul Jeffers, *The Napoleon of New York: Mayor Fiorello La Guardia* (New York: John
Wiley & Sons, 1992) 42–43.

his deep commitment to the people he served—especially workers, the poor, immigrants, ordinary citizens, and all victims of government corruption, corporate greed, the "tinhorns and chiselers," and the special "interests." A man whose stature came from his integrity and dedication, the "little Flower" (a direct translation of his first name) spent his career as champion of the underdog.

Fiorello Enrico La Guardia (the "Enrico" was later Americanized to "Henry") was born in New York City on December 11, 1882. His father, Achille, was an Italian musician; his mother, Irene Coen Luzzato, was an Italian of Jewish origin from Trieste, Austria-Hungary. In 1880, the couple sailed for America, where they had first a daughter, Gemma, and then a son, Fiorello.

Unable to find steady work in New York, Achille joined the US Army as a band master. The Army transferred the family a number of times, to North Dakota, Arizona, and Missouri. As Fiorello grew, he took in experiences that would shape his thinking as a public servant. One of these was the way Indian agents in Arizona cheated the very people they were supposed to be serving. "This was," Fiorello later noted, "my first contact with 'politicians,'" a term he equated with payoffs, corruption, and graft, a term he would never allow to be attached to himself.

A second experience revolved around his father. Just before being shipped out to Cuba during the Spanish-American war, Achille became sick, presumably from eating rotten meat. Fiorello learned that it was quite common for profiteers to sell the Army tainted food[3] and inferior equipment. Years later, as soon as he entered Congress, Fiorello proposed a bill authorizing the death penalty for anyone found guilty of perpetrating such atrocities on the US Army and its soldiers.

After Achille's death, Irene was at first denied her husband's pension because, as she was told, his death was not service-related.[4] After pleading her case, she was given a pension of $8.00 per month. She took the children back to Trieste.

---

[3]Jeffers 44.
[4]Bayor 13.

Beginning to Serve

In 1901, when he was 19, Fiorello La Guardia took a job with the US Consular Service in Austria-Hungary. His primary tasks involved helping people prepare to emigrate to America. To do that job well, La Guardia was told, he should learn the language of the people he served. Working on his own and by reading newspapers and magazines, he soon could converse in German, Croation, Hungarian, Italian, Yiddish, and English.

In this job, he realized that many families were turned back once they reached America because of health conditions. Why, La Guardia reasoned, are these people not examined before they embark on this arduous journey, only to be turned away? When one ship's captain rejected the idea of pre-boarding examinations because they would delay departure, La Guardia used his authority to hold the ship indefinitely. The captain complied.[5] This was not the last time that La Guardia would "pull rank" in the name of people who needed help.

In 1907, La Guardia returned to New York and put his language skills to work as an interpreter, first at Ellis Island where immigrants were processed, and then at the city's night courts. He tried to help immigrants navigate the sometimes contradictory provisions of admittance. He saw the slums where the immigrants went to live in the city. He saw close up the Tammany political machine's abuse and corruption, as well as the graft in the police department and among city officials. He saw, for example, the racket known as "white slavery," in which women were brought to the United States and required to repay their "sponsors" the cost of their passage by engaging in prostitution. He also saw arrests and threats of deportation as just another racket to "line the pockets of the police, lawyers, and judges, almost all of whom served political bosses of Tammany Hall.[6]

The People's Lawyer

While he worked these jobs, La Guardia attended NYU Law School. Graduating in 1910, he rented space in the offices of a Greenwich Village law firm. His reputation spread quickly as one who not only knew the lan-

---

[5]Jeffers 27.
[6]Jeffers 33.

guages of immigrants but also showed a willingness to help them. In addition, he took on the cases of the poor and the working class. Soon he became known as "the people's lawyer." He fought cases challenging the landlords, employers, and a corrupt city government, against which tenants, workers, and small shopkeepers didn't stand a chance.[7] He also gave invaluable assistance to fledgling unions in their fight for better wages and working conditions in the sweatshops.

In 1915, La Guardia became a deputy attorney for New York. In two cases, one against a polluter and another against a large oyster company on Long Island, the aggressive champion of justice felt the sting of corruption. In the former case, party bosses and his superiors told him to table the suit he was filing in court. In the latter, laws were modified, freeing those large companies of regulations that smaller companies still had to follow.[8] "The interests" once again had their way.

Unable to do much as a private lawyer to fight the government corruption and corporate greed, La Guardia ran for the office of US Congressman in the 14th district of New York, a Democratic and Tammany stronghold. The Republican Party nominated La Guardia only because no one else wanted to run in a sure-to-lose campaign. La Guardia lost, but to everyone's surprise, he made a very impressive showing. His hard work campaigning, his dynamic personality, his ability to speak to "the people" convinced the party powers to give him another chance two years later. In 1916, La Guardia was elected, becoming the first Italian American in the US Congress.

Congressman La Guardia

On La Guardia's first day in Congress in April 1917, the House Speaker, Joe Cannon, called him "boy" and tried to get him to run an errand, as if he were a Congressional page. This did not deter La Guardia. He marched to the front of the chamber and took a seat in the front row. He was told that freshmen Congressmen had to sit in the rear. But even from that lowly position, he spoke out forcefully, proposing the bill threatening death to

---

[7]Jeffers 36.
[8]Jeffers 54–55.

those who sell tainted goods to the Army. The bill did not pass but La Guardia had made his powerful first impression, one that he reinforced throughout his years in Washington.[9]

Lieutenant La Guardia

When the United States entered World War I, La Guardia supported the draft and enlisted in the US Air Service. Though some Italian Americans did not like the idea of America's going to war against Italy, La Guardia let it be known where he stood: "Those who prefer Italy," he said, "should return to Italy."[10]

In the service, La Guardia was the same cantankerous mover and shaker he was back home. When his men complained about the food they were being given, Lieutenant La Guardia ordered food from local merchants and had the bills sent to the Service. When he questioned the structural soundness of a plane he and his men would be flying, he protested. Part of his protest included a threat to don his Congressman's hat and travel across America telling people their sons were made to fly unsafe aircraft. The structural changes were made.

Unions and Prohibition

After the armistice, La Guardia returned to Congress, gaining a reputation as a progressive leader. He criticized what he saw as unfair immigration restrictions and fought for labor unions. He co-sponsored the Norris-La Guardia Act, which restricted courts from issuing injunctions to stop union activities, such as strikes.[11]

When a Congressman from Minnesota, Andrew John Volstead, proposed an 18th amendment to the Constitution to prohibit the making and selling of alcoholic beverages, La Guardia responded: "I maintain this law will be almost impossible to enforce. And if the law fails to be enforced—as it certainly will be, as it is drawn—it will create contempt and disregard for law all over the country."[12] The Volstead Act was passed, and, just as La

---

[9]Bayor 31.
[10]Jeffers 66.
[11]http://www.fiorellolaguardia.lagcc.cuny.edu/laguardia/profile2.asp
[12]Jeffers 89.

Guardia predicted, enforcement was almost impossible. In addition, pro-hibition helped spawn a new wave of crime, as gangsters selling illegal booze now had money to gain influence in other areas, including the "buy-ing" of police, judges, and other public officials.

Personal Tragedy

While serving as the "people's lawyer," La Guardia provided legal as-sistance in a strike waged by the men's garment workers union. Through his involvement he met Thea Almerigotti, a native of Trieste and a dress designer. After a five-year courtship, they married in 1919, and had a child, Fioretta Thea.

Thea had always been frail and was diagnosed with tuberculosis. Her daughter, too, was sickly from the start. To provide an environment with more open space and fresh air for his ailing wife and daughter, La Guardia pawned everything he owned and bought a house on University Avenue in the Bronx. But eventually both Thea and Fioretta were taken to a sani-tarium. On October 13, 1921, Fioretta died of spinal meningitis. Her mother was too ill to attend the funeral. Two days later, she died.[13] A few weeks after these funerals, La Guardia lost in his first bid to become Mayor of New York City. Some seven years later, he married his long-time secre-tary and political aide, Marie Fisher, with whom he adopted two children.[14]

The Mayor of New York

In 1933, La Guardia was elected Mayor of New York City, replacing the popular, dapper, and corrupt James J. Walker, known to one and all as "Jimmy." In control of the Tammany machine for years, Walker gave out hundreds of patronage jobs—in return for kickbacks and votes. There were names on the city payroll of people who had died years before. All important contracts went through Walker, with the expected cash for the mayor. He negotiated a franchise for a bus company—owned by some politicians—that had no buses. He attended every opening night on Broad-

---

[13]Jeffers, pp. 101–02.
[14]http://www.fiorellolaguardia.lagcc.cuny.edu/laguardia/profile2.asp

way and had the Central Park Casino built as a gathering space for himself and his society friends. Walker had a secret bank account that was said to contain over a million dollars.[15]

The New York that La Guardia inherited from Walker was in shambles.

> Corruption was rife and bankruptcy was imminent . . . the city was on the brink of economic collapse because of mismanagement combined with decreasing tax revenue and increasing relief requirements. (The entire country was feeling the effects of an economic depression.) The city's infrastructure had been allowed to deteriorate.[16]

The city's budget was unbalanced causing, among other things, a poor credit rating that made municipal bonds difficult to sell and that disqualified the city for federal relief funds.[17]

Taking Action

One of the first actions La Guardia took as Mayor was to "clean house" of the "clubhouse loafers" and other "hangers-on" who were drawing salaries from the city but doing nothing. La Guardia's Department of Investigations unearthed a number of problems of this type. Personnel in the Department of Purchase worked a deal with coal sellers to defraud the city on the amount of coal delivered. At the city's home for the elderly, Tammany supervisors cheated the residents of the little money they had. In Queens, developers paid off politicians to avoid adhering to city building codes. Investigations found one city worker who had not shown up for work in 11 years. La Guardia quickly fired those found out to be the perpetrators and replaced them not with political cronies but with the "best-qualified people" regardless of party. He reformed the civil service exam so the people scoring highest would get the jobs.

Besides working to rid the city of corruption, La Guardia sought efficiency, eliminating shoddy practices. The Mayor would often show up unannounced at city work stations and agencies at any hour of the day to

---

[15]Bayor 88–90.
[16]Bayor 90.
[17]Bayor 119.

see how things were going. In one case, he got in line at a relief station and found only one staff member interviewing applicants while a dozen other attendants just lounged around. The Mayor stood on line for some time, then stormed to the head of the line. "Where the hell do you think you're going?" the attendant shouted. La Guardia seized the man by the shoulders and tossed him aside as another attendant approached. Finally people recognized who he was and backed off. But he continued into the office of the director and blew up when the director was not there. He ordered a secretary to get the Welfare Commissioner on the phone at once. To the shocked attendants he said, "Let me see how fast you can clear up this crowd of applicants." They flew into action and processed all applicants in about 30 minutes. The applicants lined up outside and gave "Hizzoner" a cheer as he left.[18]

Building with Federal Money

To improve the city's financial condition, La Guardia proposed the Emergency Economy Bill, which gave the Board of Estimate special powers. Costs were cut by streamlining city bureaucracy and reducing salaries of most city workers, including the mayor's. (La Guardia, at his own request, had his salary cut from $40,000 to $22,500, and did not receive a salary increase during his 12 years in office.) The effect of the legislation was to reduce the city budget by $14 million and cut the projected 1934 budget deficit in half.[19]

With the city in a better financial position, it was able to take advantage of grants and loans from the Civil Works Administration and the Public Works Administration. New Yorkers were back to work on projects such as building the Tri-Borough Bridge, the West Side Highway Expansion, the Holland Tunnel, and the Brooklyn Battery Tunnel. The subway system was unified and enlarged. New schools, hospitals, parks, and housing were constructed. New sewage disposal plants were built that helped eliminate pollution of rivers and beaches. The High School of Art and Design was built, the first such school in the nation. And plans for two airports were put in

---

[18]Jeffers 180–81.
[19]Bayor 119–20.

motion. La Guardia had much to do personally with gathering federal funds for such projects. President Franklin Delano Roosevelt said of the Mayor: "He comes to Washington and tells me a sad story. The tears run down my cheeks and tears run down his cheeks and the first thing I know he has wrangled another $50,000,000."[20]

Another Form of Service

La Guardia chose not to wear his Jewish heritage on his sleeve, but when issues of Jewish interest came up, he was an ardent advocate for Jewish rights. As mayor, he was one of Hitler's most outspoken opponents.[21] During World War II, La Guardia served as President Roosevelt's Director of the Office of Civilian Defense, creating a number of national programs, including rationing. After the war he was appointed Director General of the United Nations Relief and Rehabilitation Administration, providing food, clothing, and shelter to millions of Europeans affected by the war. He traveled widely and met thousands of displaced persons, giving as much aid as he could muster, especially to the children.[22] Though he needed no additional incentive for this work, La Guardia had a very personal contact with the tragic effects of the war. His sister, Gemma, who had remained in Hungary when La Guardia returned to America, was held in a Nazi concentration camp, where her husband died. La Guardia eventually was able to bring her to the United States.

Farewell to "Hizzoner"

After 12 years as Mayor of New York City, "Hizzoner" decided not to run for a fourth term. On September 20, 1947, La Guardia died of pancreatic cancer. His total assets amounted to a mortgaged house and $8,000.00 in war bonds.[23] But he left a legacy that millions enjoyed for many years.

Thousands lined the streets in silence as La Guardia's funeral procession went by, and tributes came in from all corners of the country. One historian summed up La Guardia in this way:

---

[20]Bayor 119–24.
[21]http://www.jewishvirtuallibrary.org/jsource/biography/LaGuardia.html
[22]http://www.fiorellolaguardia.lagcc.cuny.edu/laguardia/profile2.asp
[23]Bayor 187.

He was an exemplary mayor and a leading reform and ethnic figure who fought valiantly over many years to create an honest, responsive city government, improve the lives of the common people, and provide representation for the new immigrant groups.[24]

---

[24]Bayor 194.

Photo: http://bioguide.congress.gov/scripts/biodisplay

FATHER VINCENT R. CAPODANNO
US Navy Chaplain

"*Some time late afternoon we heard scattered fire, we stopped close to a small hill. . . . We ran some, walked some and approached the top of the Hill and the carnage started. All I can remember is Sgt. Pete screaming 'Get that gun' and I was hit in the left arm that spun me to the ground, another shot shattered my rifle. I was screaming, along with other members of my squad, we were shot at every move we made. The machine gun was close, 15 to 25 yards away, in a thicket, part way down the far slop of the small hill or knoll I called it. This [is] very hard for me. I can remember seeing the North Vietnamese troops moving and coming toward me, there were Marines lying all around me, and I was calling for help, while with every beat of my fast pumping heart, my life blood was spurting on the ground. I could hear someone holler "Corpsman," but everytime I would move, that gun would start shooting at me, and the other Marines. At a distance I could see Doc Leal moving from Marine to Marine, and he was looking at me. I knew I was going to die, I was not able to defend myself, and the NVA were coming after me, that was my fear.*

Through all the noise and hearing myself screaming, someone touched me. I had rolled myself on my left side to put pressure on my left arm and elbow, and someone touched me, it was Fr. Vince. As I looked into his eyes, all things got silent. Not a sound could be heard. No screaming, nothing but the sound of his soft voice, and the look of compassion in his eyes. 'Stay calm Marine, someone will be here to help, God is with all of us this day!' I could see Sgt. Peters laying on the ground, blood coming from his mouth, Corpsman Leal moving in my direction, but I was not scared any longer. I was at peace. Fr. Vince was bare headed, blood on his face and neck, his right hand was mangled with a bloody compress hastily attached. He cupped the back of my head in an attempt to raise me off my arm, when all of a sudden I heard a scream, 'my leg, my leg,' and I was back in the war. I glanced over and

Corpsman Leal was sitting on the ground screaming about 25 feet from me. Fr. Vince blessed me with his good hand and leaped up and darted to Corpsman Leal. I had come to my senses and was ready to fight, the words 'get that gun' were still ringing in my head, I made an attempt to move when the gun opened up once more, not at me, but had caught Fr. Vince and Corpsman Leal and ended their lives, a long burst killed my savior and my friends."[1]

Corporal Ray Harton, US Marine

Following a Different Path

Vincent R. Capodanno was born February 13, 1929, in Staten Island, New York, the 10th child of his American-born mother, Rachel, and his Italian immigrant father, Vincent, Sr. When Vincent, Jr. was only ten years old, his father, a dockworker, died at the age of 53.

In 1949, after attending Fordham University for a year, Vincent entered the Maryknoll Missionary seminary. He chose the Maryknolls because of their work in missionaries overseas, particularly in China and Korea. After his ordination as a priest, he was assigned to work with aboriginal Taiwanese in a mountain parish in Taiwan. Seven years later, he was assigned to Hong Kong to work in a school. But Father Capodanno had other ambitions. He asked to be reassigned as a United States Navy Chaplain serving with the US Marines. In 1966, after training, he reported to the 7th Marines, in Vietnam. His tour was for 12 months, but when that tour was up, he asked for an extension and was assigned for another six months.[2]

Making a Difference

Marines who knew him have spoken unabashedly about their admiration of and love for Father Capodanno and the impact that he had on their lives.

I have a very special place in my heart for Father Capodanno. From the first day I met him, I knew he was a Chaplain for the field Marine.... It

---

[1]http://www.sescurenet.net/3rdbn5th/mike35/capodannol.htm
[2]http://www.vincentcapodanno.org/index.php?option=com_content&task=blogsection&id=
. . .

was clear that Father Capodanno knew where he was needed. During the
time he was with the battalion I spent countless hours talking with him;
about faith, and just life in general; and I always found him a true inspiration. It was interesting, he never asked if I was a Catholic, and I was
not at the time. He did regularly offer me communion and his blessings
and believe me, I welcomed the comfort he provided me. Father Capodanno was always there when he was needed, and I never knew of a Marine in 3/5 who didn't say how much they loved him, and that was long
before he was killed. At the time of his death he was elevated to Saint-
hood in my eyes![3] (Byron Hill, H&S and M3/5)

A number of Fr. Capodanno's comrades shared their impressions of
him years later as efforts were underway to encourage Father's canonization as a saint in the Catholic Church. Some spoke with or wrote to Father
Daniel Mode, who put many of those comments in his book, *The Grunt
Padre: The Service and Sacrifice of Father Vincent Robert Capodanno.* Reading just a few of those comments reveals the kind of man that Father Capodanno was and what he meant to the men he soldiered with.

"Attending one of (Father's) masses was like overhearing two friends
talk," wrote Lt. Jerry G. Pendas. "He never tried to make me a Catholic but
there was clearly a special presence about him. He constantly sought out
Marines to listen to them and talk with them."[4]

Lance Cpl. John Scafidi recalls the impression Father Capodanno made
on him one particular morning as he lined up with other Marines to receive the sacraments and receive his blessing.

It carried us through the day and it has been carrying me for the last 39
years. To have someone who could help you make sense of what you
were doing was such a gift. His way of speaking reached inside me and
touched my heart. He gave us something at that moment, but he also gave

---

[3]http://www.combatwife.net/memcapodanno.htm
[4]Jem Sullivan, "Vietnam Voices Remember Fr. Capodanno as Hero, Living Saint," Special
to the *Catholic Herald,* 8/31/06.
http.www.catholicherald.com/articles/06articles/capodanno.htm

us something for the rest of our lives. He was in some ways preparing us for the rest of our lives.[5]

Combat soldiers in Vietnam typically carried 40 to 50 pounds on their backs while navigating thick jungles and swampy rice fields. Father Capodanno carried his own 40 pounds of gear as he moved from company to company ministering the sacraments. "He was not only our chaplain," Scafidi added. "He put himself under our burdens. He didn't have to be there with us. But he wanted to."[6]

Another Marine, Capt. Tony Grimm said: "Father Capodanno's ability to relate to the Marines regardless of rank was inspiring. He was in fact the presence of Christ in our midst." His homilies were "simple and direct."[7]

In reviewing Father Mode's book, writer John Horvat wrote about Father Capodanno:

> He shared his salary, rations, and cigarettes with anyone in need. He could always be counted upon for a cold soda or a book from his reading library. When Christmas came around and soldiers felt forgotten, Fr. Vincent saw to it that no Marine was without gifts which he obtained through a relentless campaign from friends and organizations all over the world.[8]

Making the Ultimate Sacrifice

At 4:30 AM, September 4, 1967 (Labor Day back in the states), in the Thang Binh District of the Que-Son Valley, elements of the 1st Battalion, 5th Marines, found a large North Vietnamese unit of approximately 2500 men, near the village of Dong Son. Operation Swift was underway. By 9:14 AM, 26 Marines were confirmed dead. Father Capodanno requested permis-

---

[5]Sullivan. http.www.catholicherald.com/articles/06articles/capodanno.htm
[6]Sullivan. http.www.catholicherald.com/articles/06articles/capodanno.htm
[7]Sullivan. http.www.catholicherald.com/articles/06articles/capodanno.htm
[8]John Horvat, "Beyond the Call of Duty," *The American Society for the Defense of Tradition, Family, and Property.*
http://www.tfp.org/TFPForum/TFPRecommends/Books/pdre.htm

sion to join the reinforcement headed toward the battle. His Marines needed him. "It's not going to be easy," he stated. For Father Capodanno, the battle proved fatal, riddled by 27 bullets of enemy gunfire.[9]

Acknowledging His Contribution

In recognition of his service and example, several chapels in various parts of the world were named in Father Capodanno's honor, as was a US Navy fast frigate. He received many decorations, including the Bronze Star for Valor. Father Mode said recently: "I think that the most touching memorial, the one that he (Father Capodanno) would like best, is the Vietnam Memorial (in Washington) because his name appears with the other 58,000 people that gave their lives."[10]

On December 27, 1968, then Secretary of the Navy Paul Ignatius notified the Capodanno family that Father Vincent would posthumously be awarded the Medal of Honor in honor of his selfless sacrifice. The official ceremony was held January 7, 1969.[11] The Medal of Honor citation for Vincent R. Capodanno, Lieutenant, US Navy. Chaplin Corps. 3d Battalion, 5th (Marines, 1st Marine Division (Rein). FMF reads:

> For conspicuous gallantry and intrepidity at the risk of his life above and beyond the call of duty as Chaplain of the 3d Battalion, in connection with operations against enemy forces. In response to reports that the 2d Platoon of M Company was in danger of being overrun by a massed enemy assaulting force, Lt. Capodanno left the relative safety of the company command post and ran through an open area raked with fire, directly to the beleaguered platoon. Disregarding the intense enemy small-arms, automatic-weapons, and mortar fire, he moved about the battlefield administering last rights to the dying and giving medical aid

[9]http://www.vincentcapodanno.org/index.php?option=com_content&task=blogsection&id=
. . .
[10]Patricica Rudy, "Fr. Mode Writes New Book on 'Grunt Padre," *Catholic Herald.*
http://www.catholicherald.com/articles/00articles/grunt.htm
[11]http://www.vincentcapodanno.org/index.php?option=com_content&task=blogsection&id
= . . .

to the wounded. When an exploding mortar round inflicted painful wounds to his arms and legs, and severed a portion of his right hand, he steadfastly refused all medical aid. Instead he directed the corpsmen to help their wounded comrades, and, with calm vigor, continued to move about the battlefield as he provided encouragement by voice and example to the valiant Marines. Upon encountering a wounded corpsman in the direct line of fire of an enemy machine gunner positioned approximately 15 yards away, Lt. Capodanno rushed in a daring attempt to aid and assist the mortally wounded corpsman. At that instant, only inches from his goal, he was struck down by a burst of machine gun fire. By his heroic conduct on the battlefield, and his inspiring example, Lt. Capodanno upheld the finest traditions of the U.S. Naval Service. He gallantly gave his life in the cause of freedom.[12]

In May 2006, Father Vincent Capodanno was publicly declared Servant of God, the first step toward canonization as a saint in the Catholic Church.[13]

[12]http://www.mishalov.com/Capodanno.html

[13]http://www.vincentcapodanno.org/index.php?option=com_content&task=blogsection&id = . . .

Photo: Dept. of the Navy—Naval Historical Center, Wash DC
http://www.history.navy.mil/photos/pers-us-c/v.capdno.htm

Angela Bambace
Labor Leader

The fire at the Triangle Shirtwaist Factory was a tragedy waiting to happen.

In 1911, the Triangle Shirtwaist Factory in New York City employed 500 people, mostly immigrant women from Italy and Eastern Europe. Some were as young as 12 years old. They sewed clothing 60 to 72 hours a week, for a weekly salary of $1.50, the equivalent of $31.00 in 2006 dollars. Housed in the three upper floors (8 through 10) of the building, the shirtwaist company was filled with flammable textiles, and the floors were littered with scraps. Open gas lamps provided illumination. Smoking was permitted.

On March 25, 1911, a fire broke out on the eighth floor. Workers on that floor and on the tenth managed to escape, but word of the fire didn't reach the ninth floor until it was too late. There were only two exit doors on the floor, and one stairwell was filled with smoke and flames, making it impassable. The other exit door was locked. The elevator was not operable. The fire department ladders could reach only the sixth floor. The single exterior fire escape collapsed under the weight of the people trying to use it. Sixty-two women died when they jumped from windows nine stories above ground to escape the heat, smoke, and flames. A number died falling down the empty elevator shaft. In all, 146 women died.[1]

The image many people have of Italian American women, particularly in most of the 20th century, puts them in the home, stirring the pot of tomato sauce or rocking infant grandchildren on their laps. While that

---

[1] http://en.wikipedia.org/wiki/Triangle_Shirtwaist_Factory_fire

image is accurate for many, what is missing is the portrait of Italian American women in the workforce. It was not uncommon for these women—immigrants as well as first- and second-generation daughters and granddaughters of immigrants—to work outside the home. Some women held these jobs in addition to a full round of cooking, cleaning, ironing, and tending to the children.

Speaking little English, knowing nothing about rights, and having no organized "clout," many women workers became easy victims of unscrupulous businesses. Poor working conditions, long hours, and little pay were offered on a "take-it-or-leave-it" basis. Many, such as those who died tragically in the Triangle Shirtwaist Factory fire, took what was offered. Some women took action instead.

A Voice for the People

One of these women of action[2] was an Italian American named Angela Bambace. Born in Brazil of Italian parents, Bambace came to the United States in 1904 when she was six years old. She grew up in Harlem, New York, and began working in the garment industry when she was 17.[3] Unhappy with the treatment she and her co-workers had to endure, Bambace led them in an effort to organize and stand up for their rights. She helped organize the 1919 Dressmakers and Waistmakers' strike in New York City. She later led the Amalgamated Clothing Workers Union strike in Elizabeth, New Jersey in 1932. She played a major role in 1933 when the International Ladies' Garment Workers' Union (ILGWU) called for a strike against garment shops in New York City. Between 60,000 and 70,000 dressmakers—mostly women—walked off the job.[4] Bambace organized the first women's local of the ILGWU in 1936.

Fighting the Hard Fight

Unions were gaining in strength and numbers during the 1930s, in part because of the passage of the National Industrial Recovery Act, which promised to protect workers' right to organize. This act was seen as a

---

[2]http://en.wikipedia.org/wiki/Triangle_Shirtwaist_Factory_fire
[3]http://ihrc.umn.edu/research/vitrage/all/ba/ihrc279.html
[4]http://en.wikipedia.org/wiki/International_Ladies'_Garment_Workers'_Union

means of helping fight the Great Depression of the 1930s. But many parts of the country and many companies bucked that trend.

Among textile companies, those in the South were particularly stead-fast in their opposition to unions. The ILGWU asked Bambace to use her recruiting and oratorical skills in organizing the growing numbers of tex-tile workers at plants in the South. She went, traveling by car from one small town to another. Her grandson says that because she didn't drive, she had a driver, a black man. A white woman traveling alone with a black man in the South was asking for trouble. But Bambace never flinched. She took that region's membership from virtually nothing to its peak of about 15,000 members. Because she basically carried 15,000 votes in her pocket, politicians at every level courted this aggressive woman.[5]

The Perfection Company

Perhaps her toughest assignment came in Martinsburg, West Virginia. The Perfection Garment Company had resisted the national trend toward unionized labor and had warded off union efforts for almost two decades. A family-run business, Perfection employed 400 people, mostly women. Management played on its reputation as a family-oriented company that treated each employee like family. Catering employee picnics and Christ-mas parties, the company had managed to keep the unions at bay. But the company was not without tension.

Just weeks after the attack on Pearl Harbor, one worker—Margaret Decker—was fired, ostensibly because she had joined the ILGWU. Bam-bace saw the company using the war as an excuse to hold wages to a min-imum while increasing profits. She wrote to Perfection employees, indicating they would be facing new problems at the beginning of a new season:

> . . . the new styles are going to be of a higher grade of work. They are going to sell at higher prices in the stores the same way as all other com-modities have gone up. Your employer, through a very simple trick, will

---

[5]http://www.slimman.com/Recipe_Pasta_Piselli.html

make a much greater profit from them. That trick is to pay you the old, low prices (wages) for producing a better and more valuable dress.

A Breakthrough

By 1952, 450,000 Americans were dues-paying members of the ILGWU, but at Perfection, the union could not muster enough votes to represent the company's workers. The turning point came when Perfection fired a manager somewhat sympathetic to the workers' cause. The ILGWU successfully intervened on the manager's behalf, offering assistance and counsel. The union attorney appealed the case to the National Labor Relations Board and won the manager's reinstatement, as well as $400.00 in back pay. This display of controlled force showed Perfection workers that the ILGWU could provide job and financial security. In December of 1952, employees voted overwhelmingly in favor of the ILGWU.

When the union struck in the spring of 1953, Bambace went in to negotiate. The 12-day strike ended when both parties agreed to an 18-point contract, which met basic union demands. Among these were:

- a straight-time pay raise
- an incentive bonus for piece workers
- an hourly raise for skilled workers
- an open shop
- an escalator clause based on living cost changes
- a week's vacation with pay.[6]

With little violence, the strike was settled. The union made clear its desire to cooperate with management, initiating a new era at Perfection Garment Company. The company prospered for almost 40 years, until 1991, when local and international competition forced it to close its Martinsburg plant.[7]

Bambace eventually (1956) became vice president of the ILGWU, but

---

[6]http://www.wvculture.org/hiStory/labor/perfection02.html
[7]http://www.wvculture.org/HISTORY/journal_wvh/wvh52-8.html

not before being beaten, thrown down stairs, and put in jail by forces opposed to unionization.[8]

---

[8]http://www.slimman.com/Recipe_Pasta_Piselli.html

photo: http://www.italianrap.com/italam/heroes/angela_bambace.html

GILDO "GIL" MAZZOLIN and AMALIA "AMY" MAZZOLIN
Businessman, Banker and *Businesswoman, Banker*

In 1967, longtime Chicago box manufacturer Gil Mazzolin diversified in dramatic fashion, buying a distressed bank that he had heard about while serving as a director of a bank in Highwood, Illiois. Over the next three decades, red ink turned to black and one bank turned into two. With Gil at the helm and daughter, Amy, serving as second-in-command, the father-daughter duo sold a business whose assets had increased nearly 30 fold in as many years. They also established a legacy that the chronically troubled banking industry would do well to study.

"When we took over Capital Bank," Amy Mazzolin said, *"it was in a pretty deep hole because of a series of bad loans but we dug ourselves out, person by person, company by company, and we made a nice profit when we sold the bank. Ten years later, people are still coming* up to me and telling me that no bank has ever treated them as well as Capital Bank treated them.

"We made our decisions based on the character of a person. We stood by them and worked with them to find a solution when they had a problem. I can't tell you how many people we saved from bankruptcy because we were willing to go that extra mile instead of simply closing them out. I think that had a lot to do with the fact that my father was a businessman before he was a banker. He knew what it was like to manufacture a product, collect money from customers, and weather hard times. I think that was very much a part of our success."[1]

---

[1]Contributors to this profile are Madeline Iaculin Halpern and Paul Basile, from *Fra Noi*.

Photos: *Fra Noi*

Reverse Immigration

Gildo "Gil" Mazzolin launched his core business, Rex Carton Co., in 1948 with $500 borrowed from friends. The United States was just beginning to get back on its feet after World War II. Paper rationing was still in effect, but Gil believed in himself, and rented a double storefront at Grand and Ashland Avenues to begin selling reclaimed cartons. He was married and had a young daughter, Amalia, "Amy" to provide for. "I knew I could build a business," Gil said, recalling his previous ten years of experience with two other carton companies. "I knew how the business worked and I knew I could do a better job than my competitors."

Gil was born in Chicago in 1913. In 1919, his father sent him and his mother, two sisters, and a brother back to Italy where they could live a better quality of life on the family farm in Cittadella, in the province of Padua, near Venice. In 1929, Gil returned to his birthplace to live with friends in Chicago and to pursue the American dream. "The stories in Italy about America's prosperity were irresistible to many, myself included," he said. "I remember being told that if an American found a 10 dollar bill on the sidewalk, he would kick it away, because it was just as easy to find a 20 or 50 dollar bill."

Doing Whatever It Takes

When Gil arrived in Chicago in September of 1929, the stock market had peaked at 381.17. Less than a month later, the financial house of cards came tumbling down. Two years after the historic crash, the stock market had lost nearly 90 percent of its value, triggering a panic that spread across the nation, leading to the shuttering of hundreds of banks. One day, Gil would own banks of his own. But back then, times were hard and he was willing to work at any job to get by. Fortunately, his boarding house landlady was also a friend, and agreed to run a tab that Gil would repay as he earned money. "I did everything, including carrying water on construction sites," he said. "I remember working at odd jobs on days when it was 18 degrees below zero, with cardboard in my shoes to keep away the cold."

He persevered, and in 1933 finally found a job at a carton company, earning 25 cents an hour, working 50 hours a week. "I was willing to do whatever it took to learn the business and to make a future for myself," he said. "Hard work always pays off. I worked long hours for years, and I always tell young people that the good times will come if you work as hard as you have to while you're building your business." He stayed with the company, working his way up to foreman, and then moved to a better position with more of a future at another box company, where he worked for ten years, rising to manager.

In 1948, he struck out on his own and founded Rex Carton Co., named after the ship he sailed back to America on as a young man of 16. "I made friends of customers and business associates through all my years in business, and I've been in the corrugated carton business all of my life," Gil said.

> Friendships have been responsible for my success, and friends are made by keeping promises, always paying your bills to build a good credit record, being loyal, and never saying any job is too hard or any problem too difficult to solve. Every problem has a solution, and that's how I always approached my business.

Rex Carton started with only two workers—Gil and one deliveryman. At first, Rex did no manufacturing, simply selling job lots and obsolete cartons. "We would buy used cartons and sell them at a small profit. Then we built our customer base to include new carton orders. It seemed time to make a move up to manufacturing, so in 1950 we purchased a 10,000-square-foot garage and began manufacturing our own products."

Long-standing friendships based on good business practices began to produce results. In 1966, Rex Carton had outgrown its garage/plant, and Gil plowed personal savings and a bank loan into a 110,000-square-foot factory and warehouse on the Southwest Side of the city, which has since grown to 180,000 square feet. After years of continuous profit reinvestment, the state-of-the-art facility has new docks, presses, and computer systems that enable the company to offer custom design consultation, printing, laminating, and labeling services.

With few exceptions, all of his employees have been with the company for more than 25 years. In addition to building a business from the ground up, Gil has also built a secure future for his employees through generous health-care benefits, pensions, and profit-sharing plans, engendering fierce employee loyalty. Gil currently serves as chairman of the board, with his grandson, Ron Lemar, serving as president and his nephew Salvo Arena, serving as vice president.

Amy Steps In

Gil's daughter, Amy, worked at Rex after she graduated from college, taking time off to raise a family that grew to include sons Ron and Gil and daughter Amy. When Gil acquired Capital Bank and Trust in 1967, Amy had to work her way up from the bottom. "Basically, I was the bank's go-fer," she recalled with a laugh. "I was the new kid on the block and they really didn't want me around, even though I was the daughter of the new owner. So I was in charge of fetching coffee, shredding documents, buying toilet paper . . . that sort of thing."

Like her father before her, Amy persevered, working her way up to marketing director and then vice president of Capital Bank, stepping up to president of the bank's new Westmont branch when it was acquired in 1984. Serving on the board of directors of both banks for more than a decade, she played a key role in the growth of the company. "My favorite aspect of banking was dealing with people," she recalled. "I also enjoy the challenge of growing an enterprise: that, to me, is a big accomplishment."

Giving Back

When Gil and Amy sold their banks in 1987, the two established a trust that has emerged as a charitable dynamo. Among the non-profits that receive annual pledges are:

- The University of Chicago's Cancer Research Center, which under-writes basic and clinical research programs on the causes, diagnosis, treatment, and prevention of cancer
- The University of Chicago's McClean Center, the nation's first program devoted to clinical medical ethics
- Catholic Charities' New Hope Apartments, which provides intensive case management services for homeless veterans
- The Archdiocese of Chicago's Big Shoulders Fund, which provides financial support and mentoring programs to the neediest schools in the archdiocese.

In all, more than 20 charities receive donations, large and small, from the Mazzolin trust annually. Amy also serves on the University of Chicago Cancer Research Foundation Women's Board and the board of directors of Catholic Charities.

Within the Italian American community, Gil and Amy have given generously to Villa Scalabrini; the Italian Cultural Center; and Holy Rosary Church, a traditionally Italian parish. All three institutions have bestowed person-of-the-year honors on them.

On a personal level, Amy bestows a sizeable scholarship each year to young women who are beginning their college careers. She recently began a tradition of lending her San Diego timeshare to Iraqi war veterans and their families. And the apple doesn't fall far from the tree. Amy's son Ron and daughter Amy both take time out from their busy professional schedules to participate in Chicago-area mentoring programs.

"I see absolutely no point in making a success of yourself if you don't turn around and give back to the community," Amy said. "Our heritage and our faith mandate it."

MICHAEL JOSEPH PIAZZA
Athlete

The 9/11 terrorist attacks left America stunned
and fearful. New Yorkers felt the shock especially hard,
watching the twin towers of the World Trade Center
crumble, taking the lives of thousands of their loved
ones, co-workers, and neighbors. In the days that fol-
lowed, the city that never sleeps lay dormant. The city's
leadership tried to calm fears and nudge people back to a sense of normalcy.
Broadway theaters offered discounted tickets; restaurants advertised spe-
cials; and, ten days after the attacks, the Mets returned to Shea Stadium to
play baseball.

With more than 40,000 fans in the stadium, Liza Minelli sang "New York,
New York" during the seventh-inning stretch. Diana Ross took part in the
commemorative ceremonies, as did members of the police and fire depart-
ments. New York Mayor Rudy Giuliani, usually booed at Shea because he is
a Yankee fan, was cheered heartily in recognition of his strong guidance dur-
ing and after the attacks. The fans in the stadium and the millions watching
on television turned their attention away from the heartache and focused
on the field for the game between the Mets and the Atlanta Braves.

The players on the field wrestled with their own emotions. Mike Piazza,
the Mets' hard-hitting catcher, was no exception. "To get back on the field . . ."
he said later, "we were really confused. Because we didn't think that baseball
had a place in that event. But we also knew there was a time that we had to
get on with the season, get on with our lives."

Piazza was right. As city officials and others had said, it was time, not
to forget, but to move on.

"But when we got on the field," Piazza added, "[it was] just an amazing
night; emotional night, a lot of tears. I remember just standing on the lines
for the national anthem—or, actually when the bagpipers came out, I

started praying. I said 'please, God, give me the strength to get through this.'
Because it was just so hard to hold it together."[1]

Piazza did more than hold it together in a close, well-played game. In
the eighth inning the Mets came to bat trailing 2 to 1. With a runner on base,
Piazza stepped to the plate. Like the fans in the "Casey at the Bat" poem, the
Mets fans rose and cheered, exhorting Piazza to be their hero one more time
as he had been so many times before. With the count one ball and two strikes,
Piazza swung at the next pitch and sent the ball soaring into the night, out
toward left-center field, beyond the reach of the chasing outfielder and over
the fence. Home run! The Mets took the lead. Mighty Mike, unlike Casey, gave
the fans what they so needed. Symbolically that home run spoke for millions
of New Yorkers, saying "we will rise again." Years later, after he retired from
baseball, Piazza called that experience his greatest moment in sports.

Growing Up with Baseball

Michael Joseph Piazza was born September 4, 1968, to Vince and
Veronica Piazza in Norristown, Pennsylvania. With his brothers Vince, Jr.,
Danny, Tony, and Tommy, he spent much of his time in the backyard batting
cage his father had rigged up. Summer and winter, Mike worked on his hitting in hopes of some day playing in the big leagues—his father's wish.

Vince, Sr. bought and sold things, mostly cars and land, until he made
a shrewd investment in a computer company. Growing up in Norristown
himself, Vince had a friend named Tommy Lasorda who later became manager of the Los Angeles Dodgers. When the Dodgers came to play in
Philadelphia, young Mike got to sit in the dugout and then serve as Dodger
batboy.

Mike attended Phoenixville High School but did not make the varsity
team until his junior year. But that year he led the league in home runs,
and as a senior he was league MVP, hitting over .600. Despite his success,
scouts passed over Piazza in the baseball draft. That's when Vince called
on his friend Lasorda to intercede. The Dodgers picked Mike in the 62nd
round of the 1988 draft. He was the 1390th pick overall. For a time, Mike
had to endure ribbing that he was drafted only because of Lasorda's influ-

[1]Marty Noble. "Piazza's Post 9/11 shot became iconic,"
http://newyorkmets.mlb.com/news/print.jsp?ymd=

ence—which may have been true.

The Long, Hard Road to Success

Piazza spent three years in the minor leagues, hardly a quick rise in the organization. In 1992, he was called up to the big team but played in only 21 games. But the next year he was named the Dodgers' starting catcher. He was voted Rookie of the Year, hitting .362 and 40 homers, and driving in 124 runs. From then on Piazza was recognized as one of the most powerful hitters in baseball. He hit over .300 in nine consecutive seasons. He played in the All Star game numerous times and was voted MVP in the 1996 game. He is generally recognized as the top hitting catcher of all time, having hit more home runs than any other. Traded to the Mets in 1998, he led the team to the playoffs two years in a row and to the World Series.[2]

Giving Back

A gentleman on and off the field, Piazza gave back in many ways. In 1995, when he was just starting out with the Dodgers, he donated $100 for every home run he hit to a fund for all the Dodger Stadium employees who were not paid during the baseball strike. From 1994 to 2004, he played in the Annual Pepsi All-Star Game to raise money for the International Juvenile Diabetes. As a contestant on the television game show "Jeopardy," Piazza won $15,000 for teammate Al Leiter's charitable foundation called Leiters Landing. From 1998 to 2001, he donated more than $100,000 to the Mets' "Takin' it to the Fields" program to help Youth Baseball Leagues repair and improve their playing fields.

Not all of his contributions have been publicized but they are not overlooked. Piazza was honored by the Police Athletic League for his contributions to the community and received the "Good Guy" Award from the New York Chapter of the Baseball Writers Association. He toured Europe for Major League Baseball International, hosting numerous clinics for chil-

---

[2]http://www.nationmaster.com/encyclopedia/Mike-Piazza%23Personal-life

dren.[3] On the night of his post 9/11 home run, Piazza—like all the Mets—donated his paycheck to the relief effort. Piazza's donation totaled $68,000.[4]

After visiting "Ground Zero" at the demolished World Trade Center, Piazza was so touched he wanted to do something more to help. One of the firehouses, Ladder 3, put him in touch with the Carroll family. Mike Carroll was among the New York firefighters who lost his life in the World Trade Center. Carroll was a huge Piazza fan and was teaching his son, Brendan, to hit like Piazza, according to an article in *Sports Illustrated.* The day before Thanksgiving, about two months after 9/11, Piazza met with young Brendan and his mother, Nancy. Brendan was ecstatic asking questions of his and his father's favorite ballplayer. Telling Piazza that he and his dad were at the game when Piazza was hit in the head by a pitch, the boy broke down and cried.

According to the *SI* article, Piazza didn't move, but rubbed Brendan's shoulders saying, "You'll be all right, Buddy, you'll be all right." He then invited Brendan and his mother back to his place to "hang out." Nancy later said: "Brendan is hanging out with Mike Piazza, in Mike Piazza's apartment, and Mike thinks it's the funniest thing in the world."[5]

Some real-life heroes are like that.

[3]http://atlcardinals.scout.com/a.z?s=321&p=8&c=1&nid=1771496
[4]"Mike Piazza—Piazza Is Everywhere,"
http://sports.jrank.org/pages/3730/Piazza-Mike-Piazza-Everywhere.html
[5]"Mike Piazza—Piazza Is Everywhere."

Photo: Wikipedia.

LEONARD COVELLO
Educator

The first school Leonard Covello attended in the United States was known as the "Soup School," or as his father referred to it, "La Soupa Scuola." The Soup School was a three-story wooden building hemmed in by two five-story tenements at 116th Street and Second Avenue in New York City. It was called the Soup School because at lunchtime each student received a bowl of soup with, as Covello recalls, "some white, soft bread that made better spitballs than eating in comparison with the substantial and solid homemade bread to which I was accustomed."[1] Run by the Female Guardian Society of America, the Soup School's primary mission was the "Americanization" of immigrant children.

While "Americanization" of immigrant children was a worthy educational objective, the schools and teachers often pursued it to the extreme, alienating students from their native languages and cultures. When Leonard brought home a report card, his father noticed a different spelling of the family name. "What is this 'Leonard Covello?'" the father exclaimed. "What happened to the i in Coviello? From Leonardo to Leonard I can follow," the perplexed man said. "A perfectly natural process. In America anything can happen and does happen. But you don't change a family name. A name is a name. What happened to the i?" Leonard explained that his teacher took it out. "Every time she pronounced Coviello, it came out Covello. So she took out the i. That way it's easier for everybody."[2] That was Covello's first glimpse into "Americanization."

---

[1]Leonard Covello, with Guido D'Agostino, *The Heart Is the Teacher* (New York: McGraw-Hill, 1958) 22.

[2]Jack Dougherty, *Learning to Forget: A Rite of Adolescence?* (The Johns Hopkins University Press).

http://muse.jhu.edu/login?uri=/journals/reviews_in_american_history/v034/34.2doughert

From Avigliano to America

Born in Avigliano in the Basilicata region of Southern Italy in 1887, Leonardo and his family came to America in 1896, to live in the rough and tumble East Harlem section of New York City. His first home was a "tenement flat near the East River. . . . The sunlight and fresh air of our mountain home . . . were replaced by four walls and people over and under and on all sides of us. . . . The traffic of wagons and carts and carriages and the clopping of horses' hoofs which struck sparks in the night. The smell of the river at ebb tide. Dank hallways. Long flights of wooden stairs and the toilet in the hall."[3]

He took his first regular paying job when he was 12 years old. It required his getting up at five o'clock in the morning six days a week to deliver bread. His salary: $1.75 a week.[4]

At the Soup School, the teaching method was repetition, and children would learn to memorize and recite—whether they understood what they were saying or not. Covello said later this fallacy was particularly evident at assemblies, where he would sing "Tree cheers for the Red, Whatzen, Blu."[5]

Americanization: The Double-Edged Sword

Americanization as the goal of education did not stop at the Soup School. That was also the primary mission of P.S. 83, where Covello finished elementary school, as well as of Morris High School. He was given no choice of courses so the language he studied throughout those years was German. "I do not recall one mention of Italy or the Italian language or what famous Italians had done in the world," he said. . . . "We soon got the idea that 'Italian' meant inferior, and a barrier was erected between children of Italian origin and their parents. . . . We were becoming Americans by learning how to be ashamed of our parents."[6] At 17, Covello quit school to enter the work force.

---

[3]Covello, p. 21.
[4]Covello, p. 37.
[5]www.myitalianharlem.com
[6]Covello, pp. 43-44.

Gaining a New Perspective

Work was truly an eye-opener for Covello. He met people from different nationalities and came to think more favorably about the Irish, the Poles, and the Jews. "I found out," he said later, "that New York did not consist of merely Americans and Italians, but rather of people in varying stages of the thing called Americanization. ... I began to find myself reacting differently toward the bustling humanity around me." Work was for Covello an important means of crossing physical and cultural boundaries—something he had not seen happening in his years in public schools.[7]

After a year, Covello returned to high school, more confident and involved. He was particularly concerned about social injustice, but teachers cautioned him about discussing or writing about it in school. That's strange, he thought, because social injustice was something that "immigrants and negroes" faced every day. What better place than a school to discuss the issue?

Covello graduated and received a Pulitzer scholarship to Columbia University. While a student, he earned extra money teaching Italian immigrants to speak English. Though older, they would ask his advice about situations their children were facing. "It was then that I realized," Covello wrote, "how little these parents understood about school conditions and regulations affecting their children."[8]

After graduating from Columbia in 1911 and working at various jobs for two years, he took a position as teacher of French in DeWitt Clinton High School, where his students were of many nationalities. He saw that teaching adolescents involved so much more than the rudiments of a foreign language. But how could he reach them if he didn't know anything about them—their families, their lives outside of school? Before he could find out, however, World War I intervened.

He enlisted in the U.S. Army Artillery Corps and served in France as an instructor, an interpreter, and member of the Corps of Intelligence Police. In the service he met a man who, in private life, was in advertising.

---

[7]Vito Perrone, *Leonard Covello: Teacher with a Heart* (Teachers College P, 1998) 80.
[8]Covello 77.

After the war, Covello went to work for him, making more money than he had ever seen. But the challenge of what he had started in East Harlem drew him back. In 1920, Covello returned to the faculty at DeWitt Clinton High School.

Easing the Transition

Back in the classroom and serving a heavily immigrant student population, Covello became ever more aware of his own experience as a young immigrant. He saw the dilemma facing immigrant children. "They were expected to separate themselves from their native culture and language, including their families and communities, in order to meet the school's expectations and to achieve academically."[9]

Covello tried to help students manage that delicate balance. He worked at easing the transition of immigrant school children into American life without distancing them from their families and communities. He established *Il Circolo Italiano* at DeWitt Clinton, a club that involved students in American activities, combining social service, recreational, and cultural activities, many of them within the Italian immigrant community. He also began a campaign to raise the study of the Italian language in the city's schools to the level of other languages being taught. Covello was a major force in founding the Italian Teachers Association as well as the Casa Italiana Educational Bureau, a storehouse of useful information for and about the immigrants. Through his associations with most of the Italian organizations in the city, Covello tried to soften the jolt of Americanization while spreading pride in and knowledge of Italian culture.

Focus on the Community

During his tenure at DeWitt Clinton, Covello saw the need for a high school in East Harlem, a community of roughly 250,000 people. His efforts led to the creation of Benjamin Franklin High School in 1934, with Covello as its first principal. In that position Covello was able to implement his vision of a community-centered school. The public school was the one social

[9]Register of the Papers of Leonard Covello, The Balch Institute for Ethnic Studies of The Historical Society of Pennsylvania,
http://www.balchinstitute.org/manuscript_guide/html/covello.html.

agency that touched nearly all families, and the school became the educational, civic, and social center of the community.

Many students were active in helping immigrants with the English language, readying them for the citizenship test and the whole naturalization
process. Such activities gave students a larger measure of responsibility,
an important place in the intergenerational world. "The young adult," Covello often said, "is happiest when occupied at some task in the service of
his family or society."[10] "We achieved," Covello added, "what we felt should
be one of the basic aims of education—the improvement of community
life, not merely through discussion but through a demonstration of school-
community action."[11]

The school's Community Advisory Council, consisting of teachers, students, parents, and business and civic leaders, launched a program to
strengthen the East Harlem community and aid its development. The program included housing, healthcare, and sanitation campaigns; the establishment of libraries and social centers in the neighborhoods; adult
education; and summer school programs. Council members cleaned up
and renovated empty neighborhood stores and turned them into class-
rooms for adult immigrants too shy to enter the high school.[12] By special
decree of the Board of Education, Benjamin Franklin High School would
be open "every hour of every day of the year" to provide educational, cultural, recreational, social, and health services to the residents of this highly
stressed district.[13] The community-centered school—the interconnected-
ness between school and the real world—was firmly entrenched as the
guiding principle of Benjamin Franklin High School.

To Live Among the People

Covello lived in East Harlem while working there because he felt the
importance of living in the community where his students lived. Many important conversations, he later said, took place in chance encounters outside of school or in his visits to students' homes.

---

[10]Covello 155.

[11]Covello 254.

[12]Register of the Papers of Leonard Covello.

[13]Michael C. Johanek and John L. Puckett, "Leonard Covello and the Making of Benjamin
Franklin High School," www.temple.edu/tempress/chapters_1800/1857_ch1.pdf

Covello tells the story of Joe D'Angelo, a student at Benjamin Franklin, who came to him with a problem. His father, the boy said, often hit him. Not only were the blows hard, but the boy was afraid one day he might strike back. Unbeknown to his father, the boy had been boxing, and became quite good. So his fears of what could happen were serious. Covello paid a visit to the home. Sipping a glass of wine, he explained calmly—and mostly in Italian—the boy's predicament. At first the father became angry that his son would engage in boxing while telling the family he worked at a factory, but eventually he began to smile. "The smile broadened into a grin. '*That lilla sonamangonia!*' he said." That ended the use of violent hands in the D'Angelo home.

Another student, Nat, had an older brother who was mixed up with mobsters and was shot and killed. Covello went to the funeral and was criticized for doing so by some people who felt a principal should not be attending the funeral of a hoodlum. "But a few days later," Covello wrote, "Nat came and thanked me personally for going to his brother's wake. He held his cap, twisting it in his hands. 'I was gonna go after them myself,' he blurted. 'I'd a killed somebody. Then when I saw you there talking to my mother and father, I wasn't so sure any more.'"[14]

The Academic Curriculum

By 1938, the school's curriculum, in every subject field, had intercultural content. In the English Department, along with Shakespeare and Milton and Scott, students read writers such as Upton Sinclair, Lincoln Steffens, and Ida Tarbell, who dealt with contemporary social problems.[15] Each student was required to select a problem and follow it through. Those studying the problem of the slums were expected to personally investigate actual slum conditions. The group studying the problems of the "melting pot" had to find out through actual observation how people endured racial animosity. Each student had to turn in a midterm theme and a final term theme showing his personal reaction to the problem studied.[16]

---

[14]Covello 186.
[15]Perrone 205–06.
[16]Perrone 86.

Work in the Art Department also had a community focus. In too many city schools, Covello said, the artwork produced by students depicted a woodland scene, a landscape, or a seascape. Art, like poetry, was treated as something apart from the reality of daily living. "We tried to get away from this at Franklin. There, art study tied in closely with our concern with the community. What many of the boys produced, as an expression of themselves, reflected their thoughts and ideas about the daily business of living in East Harlem."

For example, instead of a waterfall with a mill, a painting would show a mud-colored brick tenement with ugly fire escapes and laundry hanging on the roof; but on the front stoop, men in shirt sleeves caught a moment of sunlight. Instead of the surf and the rock-bound coast of Maine, a charcoal sketch showed a dock on the East River and tugboats and kids swimming. It was vital art, and alive. In the midst of squalor it spoke of the yearning for a better life.

The Art Department worked out a huge map of East Harlem, carefully outlining individual blocks. The map showed that in East Harlem there were 41 churches and missions, 22 political clubs, nine labor organizations, 506 candy stores, 262 barber shops. There were 28 liquor stores, 156 bars, 26 junk shops, 685 grocers, 378 restaurants, 232 tailors, and 63 radio repair shops, as well as 297 doctors, 74 dentists, 102 furniture stores, and 14 loan offices. "It was both significant and depressing, both to students and to us teachers, that a community which could support 41 religious institutions and 22 political clubs could boast only a few open playgrounds for its children, three public halls, no neighborhood newspaper at all."[17]

Students responded in many ways. For example, some led the campaign to create a local newspaper. They gathered and wrote the news—with some stories in Italian and Spanish as well as English—coordinated contributions by adults, sold ads, and distributed the *East Harlem News*.[18]

------

[17]Perrone 205–06.
[18]Covello 231–33.

Meeting the Current Need

Many different immigrant groups settled in East Harlem. At one point, students at Benjamin Franklin High School represented 34 different nationalities. As many Puerto Rican immigrants were finding their way to East Harlem, Covello implemented programs for Puerto Rican immigrants at Franklin similar to those that had proven successful among Italian immigrants.[19]

After 45 years in education, Covello retired from the public school system. But he kept giving. He became deeply involved helping senior citizens in East Harlem, and he was a founder of the East Harlem Day Care Center for Older Persons. In 1969, the center's name was changed to the Leonard Covello Senior Center for East Harlem.[20]

---

[19]Register of the Papers of Leonard Covello.
[20]Register of the Papers of Leonard Covello.

RITA LEVI-MONTALCINI
Physician, Researcher

"I told Mother of my decision to study medicine. She encouraged me to speak to Father. . . . I began in a roundabout way. . . . He listened, looking at me with that serious and penetrating gaze of his that caused me such trepidation, and asked whether I knew what I wanted to do. I told him how much Giovanna's (her governess) death had shaken me and how I was convinced that the profession I wanted to follow was that of medical doctor. . . . He objected that it was a long and difficult course of study, unsuitable for a woman. Since I had finished school three years previously, it would not be easy to take it up again. I assured him that I was not afraid of that. With the help of a tutor, I would study privately. 'If this is what you want,' he replied, 'then I won't stand in your way, even if I'm doubtful of your choice.'"[1]

Overcoming her father's Victorian concept of a woman's role would not be the last obstacle Rita Levi-Montalcini would have to clear in her quest to serve humanity.

Rita Levi-Montalcini, with her twin sister Paola, was the youngest of the four children of Adamo Levi, an engineer, and Adele Montalcini, a painter. Born in Turin, Italy, in 1909, Rita grew up in a cultivated Jewish household, yet one in which the role of women was simply to care for husband and family. After elementary school, while her brother Gino attended high school to prepare for college, Rita and her sisters went to a school for girls, from which few graduates would qualify for college acceptance.

---

[1]Rita Levi-Montalcini, *In Praise of Imperfection: My Life and Work* (New York: Sloan Foundation Science Series, 1988). http://query.nttimes.com/gst/fulpage.html?res

"The ideal for my father," Levi-Montalcini wrote, "was my mother: exceedingly beautiful, intelligent, refined, but submissive to him, accepting of being number two. He made every decision."[2] After finishing secondary school, Rita's brother, Gino, went on to the university to study architecture.[3] One sister, Nina, married and raised a family, and Paola—like her mother—focused on painting, which was acceptable. Rita, not interested in sports or a social life that revolved around finding a husband, was unhappy.

Passionate About Research

It was then that her former governess and a longtime friend of the family, Giovanna, was diagnosed with cancer. As she watched her friend weaken and die, Rita became even more committed to becoming a medical doctor. She kept at her father for two years, and ultimately, he relented. With her cousin Eugenia, she spent a year studying Latin, Greek, and mathematics with tutors. On their own, the two girls studied philosophy, literature, and history. In 1930, both Rita and Eugenia enrolled in Turin University Medical School. They were two of only seven women among the 300 students in the Institute of Anatomy at the Medical School.[4]

Working with chicken embryos, Levi-Montalcini and her cousin conducted research on the formation of reticular fibers, situated primarily in the brain stem. She began to perfect a technique that later was so important in her discovery of the Nerve Growth Factor. "For the first time," she wrote," I became passionate about research."[5]

She also became interested in a young man who proposed marriage to her. This took a great deal of courage on his part because he was not Jewish, and anti-Jewish laws were becoming the norm in Italy. The issue of whether or not to marry was made moot, however, by a decree prohibiting marriage between Jews and Caucasian non-Jews ("Aryans").[6]

---

[2] Ruby Rohrlich, "Jewish Lives: Rita Levi-Montalcini," p. 2. http://findarticles.com/p/articles/mi_m0411/is_1_49ai_61887407/
[3] Rita Levi-Montalcini, *In Praise of Imperfection: My Life and Work* 2.
[4] Rohrlich 4.
[5] Rohrlich 5.
[6] Rohrlich 5.

Restricted by the Manifesto

Levi-Montalcini graduated at the top of her class in 1936 and took a position as assistant lecturer in the Anatomy Department. But that assignment was short-lived as she was dismissed when Benito Mussolini issued the "Manifesto per la Difeza della Razza," barring academic and professional careers to non-Aryan Italian citizens. Levi-Montalcini responded by taking a research position at a neurology institute in Brussels, but the threat of a German invasion of Belgium caused her to return to Italy.

At first she practiced medicine surreptitiously for the poor people of Turin without charging fees, but the need to have "Aryan" doctors sign prescriptions put an end to that work. She then set up a small laboratory in her bedroom at home so she could continue her research, improvising when she could not purchase actual laboratory equipment.[7] She studied chicken embryos to determine the effect that amputations of limbs have on the nervous system. In 1942 she wrote an article describing her research and her findings. The article was published in a professional journal and would later prove to be a catalyst to her career.

Continuing the Research

After Italy entered the war and the allies were bombing the northern industrial cities, Levi-Montalcini and her family moved to the highlands, about an hour from Turin. Again Levi-Montalcini set up a laboratory, this time in the corner of the dining area in a rented cottage. To gather chicken eggs for her experiments she traveled from farm to farm on bicycle. Through her research she was arriving at findings that contradicted what was written in the neuroanatomy textbooks at the time.

Levi-Montalcini's achievement, however, was overshadowed by the specter of German armies marching into Italy, bringing "the Holocaust, with its roundups, mass shootings, Gestapo interrogations, incarcerations, disappearances, and eventual deportations to extermination camps."[8]

With Turin under siege, Levi-Montalcini and some of her family tried to escape to Switzerland but were rebuffed by Italian guards at the border.

---

[7]Rohrlich 6.
[8]Rohrlich 6.

With false identity cards, they boarded a train heading south and got off at Florence. There a friend of Paola's put them up in her home, sheltering them at great risk to herself.[9]

Practicing Wartime Medicine

In September 1944, British forces liberated Florence. With many civilians and military personnel wounded and sick, Levi-Montalcini registered with the Allied Health Service at American-Anglo Headquarters. She tended to many suffering from malnutrition and cold, and she saw many newborns die from dehydration. In the overcrowded barracks used as hospitals, the water was polluted, and abdominal typhoid among the refugees reached epidemic proportions. This undertaking led to what Levi-Montalcini would later call her "most intense, exhausting, and last experience as a medical doctor."[10]

Next: USA

In July of 1945, Levi-Montalcini and her family returned to Turin. Seriously depressed by her recent experiences, Levi-Montalcini decided she would never practice medicine again. She resumed her research position in the University's School of Medicine. One summer morning she received a letter from Viktor Hamburger of Washington University in St. Louis, Missouri. He had read the article she had written some time ago and was interested in exploring further the "problem" she was working on, specifically "the effects of amputation on the development of the nervous centers in the excised limbs" of chick embryos. He offered her a position at Washington University for one semester. She accepted the invitation and headed for the United States. Building one success on another, she stayed for 30 years.[11]

At Washington University she worked closely with Dr. Stanley Cohen, a biochemist and newly appointed research associate in the biology department. Both had limited backgrounds and Cohen said: "You and I are

---

[9]Rohrlich 7.
[10]Rohrlich 7.
[11]Rohrlich 8.

good, Rita, but together we are wonderful."[12] The pair found the growth-stimulating substance, a protein found in malignant tumors that causes nerve fibers to grow rapidly. They called the substance the Nerve Growth Factor.[13] Their research was "of fundamental importance to the understanding of cell and organ growth," one reviewer wrote, "and plays a significant role in understanding cancers, birth defects, and diseases such as Alzheimer's and Parkinson's.[14] This discovery was "one of the most important steps taken toward understanding how the fantastically complex system of nerves is laid down and linked to tissues in a developing embryo."[15]

Some time later, Cohen left the University, and Levi-Montalcini began expanding her relationships outside of the University. With a grant from the National Science Foundation, she established a counterpart laboratory in Rome. Now owning dual citizenship, she spent six months a year in Rome and six months in the States. Things were going well but few scientists explored the area of her research. The results were "so perplexing and hard to reconcile with prevailing theory."[16] One positive effect of her work and recognition, however, was that many more women were choosing the sciences as a career path and entering the research laboratories.

Gaining Admiration

After many years of hard work, Levi-Montalcini began to receive the profession's attention and admiration. She was the first woman scientist to receive the Max Weinstein award, given by the United Cerebral Palsy Association for outstanding contributions in neurological research. In 1986, Levi-Montalcini received the Lasker award, the most prestigious science prize in the United States. In that same year, she and Cohen were awarded the Nobel Prize in Medicine or Physiology for their discovery of the Nerve Growth Factor. Of the 625 prizes that had been awarded in the 93-year history of the Nobel prize, women had received only 25. Of those,

---

[12]Rohrlich 8.
[13]"Rita Levi-Montalcini," http://thinkquest.org/20117/levimontalcini.html
[14]Women in Health Sciences. Rita Levi-Montalcini.
http://beckerexhibits.wustl.edu/mowihsp/bios/levi_montalcini.htm
[15]Victor K. McElheny, "As Self-Made Scientist," *New York Times* 1 May 1988: 1.
http://query.nytimes.com/gst/fulpage.html?res=940DE0D9133BF932A35756C0A96E94
[16]Rohrlich 8–9.

only five were in medicine and physiology. In addition, Levi-Montalcini was the first Italian woman to receive a Nobel prize in science.[17]

To Reach the Heart

Levi-Montalcini, though advancing in age, did not just rest on her laurels. She continued to write, ultimately publishing more than 200 articles on science and several on the social significance of science. She wrote her autobiography and a paper on the women's emancipation movement. She gave talks to adolescents in schools, urging them to face life with optimism. On her ninetieth birthday, she celebrated the publication of her new book, *Ninety Years in the Galaxy of the Mind,* which provides a system of ethics for new generations. She continued working toward her objective which was "not to disseminate scientific knowledge" as much as it was "to reach the heart of man and woman, illustrating their capacities of awareness and, therefore, of free will and responsibility."[18]

Giving Back in Other Ways

In 1992, she founded the Levi-Montalcini Foundation to assist young people in the difficult choices regarding their fields of study. In 1993, Levi-Montalcini discovered a letter from a 12-year-old Bosnian girl growing up amidst the wreckage of war. The letter was addressed to the persecuting Serbian army. She wrote: "My angry people must forgive me if I cannot hate you, because I think that we 12-year-olds have not yet fallen into the abyss of hate." Levi-Montalcini sought the girl out and had her Foundation provide a scholarship so the girl could go to school. She eventually attended Zagreb University. Levi-Montalcini wrote: "I wanted her to be an emblem of the new generations. Without hatred."[19]

Levi-Montalcini has used her celebrity to speak out on issues such as world peace and hunger. "Peace is not the absence of war," she said. "Peace is something that goes further; peace must be worked out and built."[20] She

---

[17]Rohrlich 9.
[18]Rohrlich 10.
[19]Rohrlich 11.

also was named one of the first four FAO Ambassadors by the Food and Agricultural Organization of the United Nations, to help in its campaign against world hunger. She has spent countless hours as an envoy, writing and speaking about the plight of the hungry in the world.[21]

Levi-Montalcini conceived her dream in Italy, achieved it in America, and gave back to both countries and to the world at large.

[20]"Rita Levi-Montalcini," http://www.jakvydelat.com/montalcini/
[21]"Nobel Prize Winner Rita Levi Montalcini, FAO Ambassador's Programme.
http://www.fao.org/wfd/ambas/amb/montalcini_en.htm
photo: "Rita Levi-Montalcini," http://www.jakvydelat.com/montalcinin/

Lt. Giuseppe "Joseph" Petrosino
Police Officer

On the night of March 12, 1909, Lt. Joseph Petrosino of the New York City Police Department stood in the Piazza Marina, in Salerno, Italy. He had come to Italy as part of an investigation conducted jointly by the New York City Police and Italian immigration officials. His objective was to establish the real identities and backgrounds of New York criminals and determine which ones were wanted in Italy. The intent was to have such criminals deported. As he waited beneath the statue of Garibaldi, Petrosino was gunned down. A major threat to organized crime in Italy and New York had been eradicated.

Giuseppe "Joseph" Petrosino was born in 1860 in Padula, in the province of Salerno, Campania, a village in southern Italy. When he was 14, he emigrated with his family and settled in New York City. While shining shoes near a Greenwich Village police precinct, he decided he wanted to be a policeman. But he had a few things working against him—he did not meet the height requirement, he spoke English with an accent, and he wasn't Irish. So he took work instead in the city's sanitation department, where his diligence and strong work ethic enabled him to rise quickly to the position of foreman.[1]

But Petrosino hadn't given up on his goal. As luck—or destiny—would have it, a police captain—Alexander "Clubber" Williams—was placed in charge of the street cleaning department and took a liking to Petrosino. The captain used his influence to get the authorities to overlook Pet-

---

[1]William Bryk, "The Murder of Joe Petrosino" (New York Press)
http:////www.nypress.com/15/46/news&columns/oldsmoke.cfm

rosino's inadequacies, and in 1883 Petrosino received his appointment to the police force.[2]

Fighting a Special Kind of Crime

The New York City Police Commissioner at the time was Theodore Roosevelt, who would later become United States President. He and Petrosino became friends, a relationship that would eventually become a sidelight in United States history. Roosevelt promoted Petrosino to Detective Sergeant in charge of the department's Homocide Division, the first Italian American to lead this division. Some time later, he was promoted to Lieutenant and put in charge of the newly formed Italian Squad, an elite corps of Italian American detectives. The Squad's role was to combat organizations such as the Black Hand, which had been terrorizing and extorting money from hard-working Italian Americans. Petrosino saw such organizations as disgracing Italy, Italians, and Italian Americans, and he devoted his life to fighting these groups.

He and his men used many tactics, including disguises and infiltration into the ranks of these gangs.[3] Through the Italian Squad's infiltration into an Italian-based anarchist organization, the one that had assassinated King Umberto I of Italy, Petrosino found out about a plan to assassinate United States President William McKinley in Buffalo, New York. Petrosino delivered that information to the Secret Service and his friend Theodore Roosevelt, who was then Vice President. Roosevelt vouched for Petrosino's reputation and told the president, but McKinley made the trip. On September 6, 1901, in Buffalo, Leon Czolgosz shot and killed President McKinley.[4]

Unconventional Tactics

Sometimes Petrosino used tactics that would be frowned upon today, such as threats and force. When his friend, Enrico Caruso, the great tenor,

---

[2]Bryk.

[3]"The American Mafia Crimefighters," http://www.onewal.com/maf-pol.html

[4]"Joe Petrosino," Wikipedia, http://en.wikipedia.org/wiki/Joe_Petrosino

was threatened by the Black Hand, he turned to Petrosino for help. Petrosino told Caruso to inform the extortionists he would pay the money for which they asked. When one of them came for the money, he was met by Petrosino who reportedly broke the man's legs, put him on a boat to Italy, and threatened to shoot him if he ever returned.[5]

More frequently, though, Petrosino used more conventional approaches. He recognized that it would be an error to attribute all crime against Italian Americans to a single international crime syndicate. Instead he said it was decentralized groups of individuals who were extorting money from Italian Americans. Because it was difficult to collect evidence against some of these thugs, Petrosino often sought to have them deported. By law, anyone could be deported who was wanted for a crime in Italy, or who had lied about being wanted in Italy when he immigrated to the United States.

The Ill-fated Trip

It was for this kind of information that Petrosino ventured to Italy in 1909. His trip was supposed to be top secret, but it is thought that New York's Police Commissioner, Thomas Bingham—inadvertently or intentionally—revealed Petrosino's plans to a newspaper. Word of Petrosino's expedition spread, but he made the trip anyway. In his native Italy, while serving the cause of justice, Petrosino was killed.

Days later back in New York, as his funeral cortege passed, more than 200,000 people lined the streets. They paid homage to the man who gave his life in defense of Italian Americans that had fallen victim to gangsters from among their own people.

Though his crime-fighting days were cut short, Petrosino was responsible for deportation of 500 criminals, most of whom were connected to Black Hand, and for reducing crime in New York against Italian Americans by half.[6]

---

[5]"Lt. Giuseppe "Joseph" Petrosino," http://www.mobsters.8m.com/petrosino.htm
[6]"Lt. Giuseppe "Joseph" Petrosino," http://www.mobsters.8m.com/petrosino.htm

photo: Wikipedia

MATILDA RAFFA CUOMO
Humanitarian

"Like many first-generation Americans, I missed kindergarten and began school in the first grade, as required by law. At the time, there was little interaction between families and schools, and little tolerance for non-English-speaking immigrants, like my parents. I re-  *member the pain of witnessing my mother's embarrassment when the principal brusquely ordered us to leave school because my mother was unable to fill out the enrollment forms for kindergarten. As we walked home she squeezed my hand, and I watched her eyes fill with tears of embarrassment and frustration. This memory has always reminded me of the resilience, courage, and love it took for her to raise five children."*[1]

Later, when she did register for school, an administrator changed her given name, Mattia, to the Anglicized Matilda.[2]

When she attended P.S. 137 in Brooklyn, Matilda was shy and insecure, unwilling to speak or assert herself.

"The first person to single me out for the encouragement I needed was Mrs. Kulyer, my fourth-grade teacher. She took the time to talk to me, draw me out, and share my thoughts about what I might do when I grow up. She was my first mentor beyond my parents. When Mrs. Kulyer told me I would make a great teacher, a whole world opened up. I rushed home to tell my parents the good news, and I never forgot her advice and encouragement. Years later, I was teaching second grade in a public school in Elmont, Long Island."[3]

---

[1]Matilda Raffa Cuomo, ed., *The Person Who Changed My Life* (New York: Barnes & Noble, 2002) xiv.
[2]Merrie Rosenberg, "Matilda Cuomo and Maria Cuomo Cole: A Mutual Admiration Society," *Education Update Online* (May 2001): 2.
[3]Cuomo, ed. xv.

Matilda Raffa Cuomo has dedicated her life to people in need—both as a private citizen and as wife of the long-term governor of New York State, Mario Cuomo.

Mrs. Cuomo left teaching to raise the five children she had with Mario Cuomo. They had met in the cafeteria of St. John's University in Queens, where they both earned degrees. A workaholic lawyer, Mario moved up the ranks quickly but then decided to give up his law practice for politics. Mrs. Cuomo was not happy about the loss of potential earnings.[4] Nevertheless, Mrs. Cuomo supported her husband's political ambitions while she tended to the home and children.

At the same time, she was very much involved in the community. She served as the chairwoman of the Queens chapter of the American Cancer Society. She launched the "daffodil sale" to raise funds, selling the flowers to hotels and businesses. "The daffodils were in my garage," she said. "My kids knew about my involvement. It was one of our projects every year. It was important for the children to get involved in this way."[5]

Her daughter Maria Cuomo Cole adds: "Even when we were small, we did the Boy Scouts and Girl Scouts, the American Cancer Society, and she was always organizing the community for more school enrichment programs. Of course, she did the PTA. Her service to the community was through her family, and through her church." Mrs. Cuomo believed that because her family was one generation removed from immigrants, her children understood how important it was to help those who needed help.[6]

In 1979, Mrs. Cuomo was appointed by Governor Hugh Carey to chair the New York State Committee on the International Year of the Child for UNICEF. Over the years she was invited numerous times to participate in UNICEF activities throughout the world. For example, in 1994 she delivered a keynote address for the United Nations Steering Committee at the conference in the Republic of Malta launching the International Year of the Family.

First Lady of New York

---

[4]Kevin Sack, "At Home with Matilda Raffa Cuomo: Working to Renew the Lease," *The New York Times* 21 July 1994: 1.

[5]Rosenberg 1–2.

[6]Rosenberg 2.

In 1983, her husband Mario was elected to his first of four terms as Governor of New York. While some first ladies played merely a ceremonial role, Mrs. Cuomo used the leverage of her position to work for the benefit of children and families. She has been described as "the most active First Lady in New York State's history."[7]

As First Lady from 1983 to 1995, she worked diligently as a volunteer with community leaders establishing programs to prevent child abuse, strengthen families, promote adoptions of foster care children, and prevent school dropout.

Mrs. Cuomo chaired and served as chief spokesperson for the "New York State Decade of the Child," the Governor's initiative to improve the quality of and access to more than 140 state programs for children and families. She also chaired the NYS Citizens Task Force on the Prevention of Child Abuse and Neglect. She initiated the 24-hour Parent Information Line, a computerized database of local resources that parents can access across the state. This Line still exists, though under another name, and handles 2000 calls each month.

She was instrumental in the creation of the educational program "Nutrition for Life," as well as "New York Family Album," a nationally replicated adoption recruitment tool, and "Families for Kids, ASAP," an innovative restructuring of the entire child welfare system in New York State.

Under her leadership, the New York State Health Department established a NYS parenting program—the Pre- and Post-Natal Parenting Hospital, which has been replicated in many states. PPPEHP operated in 174 New York State hospitals providing maternity services. A book entitled *Welcome to Parenthood* is distributed free in all hospitals.

Mentoring USA

In 1986, the Governor sought Matilda's counsel regarding the alarming student dropout rate in New York State. Drawing on her experiences as a child, a teacher, and a parent, Mrs. Cuomo suggested matching every at-risk student with a caring, trained volunteer. That was the beginning of the New York State Mentoring Program. Mentors worked with students

---

[7]http://www.helpusa.org/PageServer?pagename=MUSA_About_Matilda_Raffa_Cuomo

one-to-one for at least four hours a month for one year. They motivated students to stay in school, avoid drugs and teenage pregnancy, and gain self-confidence and hope. The Program drew on the support of thousands of volunteers, corporations, government, and the community. The Program served 10,000 children throughout the state.[8] Though that program was later eliminated by the next administration, in 1995 Mrs. Cuomo established Mentoring USA, which was built on the New York Program model and encouraged by her son Andrew Cuomo, former Secretary of Housing and Urban Development and currently New York State Attorney General.

Mentoring USA has expanded nationally and internationally. For example, Mentoring USA/Italia Onlus provides mentors working one-to-one for more than 700 children. The European Union has designated MUSA/Italia to bring the mentoring model to other European countries—Spain, Belgium, and Latvia.

Expanding the Reach

In response to an alarming increase in violence and hate crimes in New York City schools, Mentoring USA developed its BRAVE (Bias-Related Anti-Violence Education) Program. BRAVE encouraged children to learn about their own culture and traditions while respecting those of others.

With seed money from United Way of New York City and the Annie E. Casey Foundation, Mentoring USA brought mentoring opportunities to children in foster care. The Foster Care Initiative provided children and teenagers in foster care with the human connection that is often missing from their lives. In 2001, Mentoring USA joined forces with the Strang Cancer Prevention Center and the MetLife Foundation to implement Healthy Children Healthy Futures. This program provided children with the opportunity to learn about healthy eating and physical activity. The children were then directed and motivated to create compelling media messages encouraging their peers to adopt healthier lifestyles.[9]

Working for Peace and Understanding

---

[8]Cuomo, ed. xii–xv.
[9]Cuomo, ed. xvi–xviii.

In 1992, Mrs. Cuomo was appointed as the chairperson of the New York State Commission for the Christopher Columbus Quincentenary. With the Commission, she developed two curricula: one for Latino children and one for Italian American children, to help them appreciate and learn more about their culture and heritage.

Mrs. Cuomo has also been at the forefront of programs to promote international collaboration. Working with New York State's Director of Economic Development, Vincent Tese, and the Urban Development Corporation, she opened international offices for trade and investment, providing jobs for New York State in China, Japan, Italy, and Spain.

For more than 30 years, Mrs. Cuomo has been a national spokeswoman in the crusade to prevent breast cancer, and she has been an active participant in health-related activities. She has initiated and directed many medical conferences between the USA and Italy (C.N.R., Consiglio Nacionale delle Ricerche), with participation of NIH (National Institute of Health) and NCI (National Cancer Institute). She also coordinated a conference at the New York Academy of Medicine that involved The Brescia Medical Center, The American Cancer Society, and Memorial Sloan-Kettering Cancer Center.

Promoting Italian Studies

Always aware of the impact of and need for education, Mrs. Cuomo has also held a deep fondness for her Italian American heritage. When various organizations were pursuing the College Board to offer an Advanced Placement (AP) exam for high school students studying the Italian language, she readily stepped forward to use her influence in accomplishing this goal.

Language is the portal through which we learn and by studying the Italian language, students will come to understand, appreciate, and propagate Italian and Italian American culture.

Achieving AP status, however, is not easy. To gain its approval, the College Board insisted that the committee Mrs. Cuomo led acquire 500 high schools in the United States to teach the Italian language and to raise $500,000. This goal could be reached, Mrs. Cuomo said, only through the combined efforts of a number of individuals and organizations. Four groups in particular have been recognized for their efforts: the American

Association of Teachers of Italian, the National Italian American Foundation, the Order of the Sons of Italy in America, and UNICO National.[10]

"We are delighted," Matilda said, "that in 2008, just three years after the AP Italian exam was inaugurated, over 2,000 students took the exam. This number is striking, considering the years of study required for a successful completion of the test. This is also an increase of 23% over the 2007 participation, clearly demonstrating that there is a growing demand for one of the great languages in world history."[11]

Despite that apparent success, however, in January of 2009, College Board officials announced that the AP Italian exam would not be offered in 2009–2010. The reason: insufficient enrollment and funds. Other countries, such as China, Japan, Korea, and Russia, pay for their AP courses. The Italian Language Foundation had raised more than $650,000 in pledges and commitments, but these were made with the understanding that the Republic of Italy would at least match what the Foundation raised. That did not happen. But should the funding materialize, AP Italian may again be considered.[12]

Honors, Awards, and Personal Information
Among the many honors and awards Mrs. Cuomo has received are:

- Cum Laude Graduate of St. John's University Teachers College
- President's Medal from St. John's College and Manhattan College
- A Doctorate in Humane Letters from Siena College and St. Rose College
- The President's Medal from New York University

---

[10]Dr. Geraldine M. Chapey, "Cuomo Began AP Italian Courses," *The Wave* 17 Oct. 2003, http://www.rockawave.com/News/2003/1017/Columnists/004.html
[11]"Italian American Leaders Establish Italian Language Foundation to Support High School Studies in Italian," University of Phoenix, July 4, 2008.
http://www.reuters.com/article/pressRelease/idUS104762+04-Jul-2008=PRN20080704
[12]"College Board Says 'Arrivederci, AP Italian,'" http://www.usnews.com/blogs/on-education/2009/01/09/college-board-says-arrivederci-ap

Photo: Matilda Raffa Cuomo, Mentoring USA
http://www.helpusa.org/site/PageServer?pagename=MUSA_A_Message_from_the_Foundation

- The first Lion of Judah Award from the United Jewish Appeal Federation
- The 1997 Lifetime Achievement Award from *Family Circle* magazine

She has been married to Mario Cuomo since 1954. They have five children and 13 grandchildren.

The Volunteer's Volunteer

Always a volunteer, Mrs. Cuomo published *The Person Who Changed My Life,* a book containing accounts by 78 celebrities on their mentors—people who have had a lasting influence on their lives. All proceeds of the book go to Mentoring USA. Mrs. Cuomo is working on a new edition of the book with more celebrities. This book will be translated into Italian for MUSA/Italia.

In 1997, President William Clinton and Colin Powell, President of America's Promise, held the first Summit on Volunteerism. Whom did they ask to be guest speaker? Mrs. Cuomo—the volunteer's volunteer.

Matilda Raffa Cuomo—the epitome of the Italian American who has achieved the dream and given back.

Peter W. Rodino, Jr.
Congressman

"There was a sense of fear in the air," in the fall of 1973, said John Dean, then a top adviser to President Richard M. Nixon. Dean became a star witness in the Watergate hearings, an investigation conducted by Congress into alleged violations of principles of the Constitution by the sitting President of the United States. "When Nixon fired Archibald Cox (Watergate Special Prosecutor) it really sent a shudder through the city," Dean added. "You were talking about wiretaps,  you were talking about break-ins, you were talking about dirty tricks, you were talking about enemies (lists). That was frightening."[1]

What came to be known as the Watergate scandal began in June of 1972, when five men linked to Nixon's Committee to Re-elect the President (a Republican) had been arrested for breaking into the headquarters of the Democratic National Committee in the Watergate building in Washington, DC. Over a period of months, as journalists and others dug deeper into this event, testimony was being given and evidence uncovered indicating that top officials in the Nixon administration may have been involved in planning the break-in or in covering it up. When it was revealed that the President had tape recordings of Oval Office conversations, Watergate Special Prosecutor Cox asked for the tapes. The President refused to surrender them, citing Executive Privilege. When Cox insisted on the tapes, Nixon ordered the Attorney General, Elliot Richardson, to fire Cox. Richardson refused and resigned his position. His deputy, William Ruckelshaus, also refused but he did not resign. He was fired. The next in command, Solicitor Robert Bork, finally fired Cox. This series of events came to be known as the "Saturday Night Mas-

[1]Howard Kurtz, "A Pale Ghost of Scandals Past," *Washington Post* 3 Dec. 1998.
http://www.washingtonpost.com/wp-srv/politics/special/clinton/stories/kurtz120398.htm

sacre." Ultimately, the tapes were delivered to the new Watergate Special Prosecutor, Leon Jaworski.

This was the environment in which Hon. Peter W. Rodino, Jr., Congressman from New Jersey, found himself as Chairman of the Committee on the Judiciary, the body that would determine if the President should face impeachment.

Born Pellegrino Rodino, Jr., the son of Italian immigrant parents, he attended local public schools and the University of Newark. Rodino spent 10 years working during the day and attending law school at night to receive his law degree from Newark Law School (later Rutgers Law School). Well before the attack on Pearl Harbor, Rodino enlisted in the US Army. During World War II, he served with the United States Army from 1941 to 1946. With the First Armored Division in both Italy and North Africa, he received one of the first battlefield commissions and earned a Bronze Star, War Cross, and Knight of Order of the Crown from Italy. After the war, he ran for Congress in 1946 but was defeated in his first effort. He was elected to the 81st Congress, however, when he ran again in 1948, representing the North Ward. That was the beginning of run of 20 successful terms as a Congressman.[2]

Representing a district that was heavily Italian American during his early years in Congress, he was a strong proponent of immigration law reform. Rodino also fought for civil rights reforms. He was one of the primary sponsors of the Civil Rights Act of 1964 and the Voting Rights Act of 1964.

Rodino's ultimate successor, Rep. Don Payne (D-NJ), said that although Rodino was retiring, running for the Newark-based seat of such a revered man was no easy thing. "Payne realized that Rodino had made the residents of the blighted and poverty-stricken district proud. His constituents, now mostly African Americans, respected Rodino and knew that he respected them. Time and again, when Payne asked voters what they liked most about Rodino, the response was that Rodino respected them."[3]

---

[2]"Peter W. Rodino," Wikipedia. http://en.wikipedia.org/wiki/Peter_Rodino
[3]Ken Feltman, "Is DeLay Forgotten But Not Gone?" Inside Washington's Headlines. http://www.radnor-inc.com/inside/06/05.htm

Upon his retirement from Congress, Rodino taught at Seton Hall Law School until his death at 96.

Presiding Over the Watergate Hearings

But Rodino will forever be associated with Watergate. In Senate hearings, more and more people had revealed evidence that implicated the White House in the break-in and cover-up. Two of Nixon's closest aides, John Erhlichman and H.R. Haldeman, resigned. Dean, however, refused to resign, as he said he was "unwilling to be a scapegoat in the Watergate case."[4] Some members of the Senate called for the President's impeachment. Before that could happen, however, the House Committee on the Judiciary had to determine whether the President had acted in violation of fundamental principles of the Constitution, and if so, to undertake investigative hearings, the first step in the impeachment proceedings.

The hearings began in May of 1974. The Committee had to vote on five articles of impeachment, and it was thought the vote would go along party lines. A nasty, partisan battle was expected. It was up to Rodino to prevent such a fracas.

The World Is Watching

The stakes were indeed high. The world was watching to see if the President of the United States, elected by the people, would possibly be removed from office. Staunch supporters of Nixon, as well as many who just could not bear to see an American president ousted, lobbied for and gave testimony on Nixon's behalf. Just as vocal were those who felt no individual is above the law. It fell to Rodino, this relatively unknown from Newark and in only his first year as chairman of this Committee, to keep the televised hearings from becoming personal, political, and emotional. From the start, he set a tone of solemnity and historic significance.

Throughout all of the painstaking proceedings of this committee," Rodino said at the outset, "I as the chairman have been guided by a simple principle, the principle that the law must deal fairly with every man.

---

[4]Peter Rodino. The National Archives Learning Curve.
http://www.spartacus.schoolnet.co.uk/JFKrodino.htm

For me, this is the oldest principle of democracy. . . . Make no mistake about it. This is a turning point whatever we decide. Our judgment is not concerned with an individual but with a system of constitutional government. . . . Whatever we now decide, we must have the integrity and the decency, the will and the courage to decide rightly. Let us leave the Constitution as unimpaired for our children as our predecessors left it to us.[5]

The Verdict

The Committee ultimately agreed that the President was guilty of three of the five main charges against him—obstructing justice, abuse of power, and withholding evidence. The majority of Republicans voted with the Democrats, producing a bipartisan majority against the President.[6] Rather than see the process advance to the next level, Nixon resigned.

In Praise of the Chairman

Throughout the hearings and for years after, people praised the way Rodino kept a highly-charged event under control, the way he achieved a sense of fairness and openness in what could have become a strictly partisan vote.

Comments extolling Rodino's handling of the hearings poured in from all parts of the country. Here are some of those comments:

As the nation rocked in shame, all of us watched Chairman Rodino manage our destiny. We came to know his calmness, his strength, his sense of order. We grew to trust his honesty. We watched the citizen-politician at work, and as we watched, we rediscovered in him the best of ourselves and of this nation. Through long and bitter hours, to millions of Americans, Peter Rodino was America. (Fr. Timothy Healy, President of Georgetown University)[7]

---

[5]"The Fateful Vote to Impeach," TIME Archive.
http://www.time.com/magazine/article/0,9171,879405-5,00.html
[6]Peter Rodino, The National Archives Learning Curve.
http://www.spartacus.schoolnet.co.uk/JFKrodino.htm
[7]Fr. Timothy Healy, "Proceedings Before the Committee on the Judiciary," May 12, 1977, 95th Congress, 1st Session, House Document 95–307).
http://thomas.loc.gov/cgi-bin/ query/R?r109:FLD001:S08484

His (Rodino's) obvious integrity and steady leadership of the Committee during this period were reassuring to a nation recoiling from the complicity of a President in the perpetration of criminal acts. . . . When the nation needed a guiding hand in this national crisis, Peter Rodino steered with diligence, respect, and thoughtfulness. . . . As the chairman, Mr. Rodino ensured that the Judiciary Committee behaved responsibly. He brought his personal gravitas and respect to the hearings and guaranteed that the proceedings were respected by all. (Rep. Charles B. Rangel; D-NY)[8]

Rodino's courteous and respectful attitude set a tone that permitted the House—and the nation—to assess the facts unemotionally and to reach the necessary conclusion that President Nixon needed to go. (Rep. Don Payne; D-NJ)[9]

. . . he [Rodino] proceeded with great patience, caution, enormous energy, and fairness above all. He strove to achieve a spirit of fairness and bipartisanship . . . members of the committee drew together over the course of the inquiry, approving three articles of impeachment on strong bipartisan votes and, ultimately, reaching unanimity on the need to move the impeachment process forward. (Sen Paul S. Sarbanes; D-MD)[10]

It is a testament to the man that, when the vote to impeach was rendered, rather than grandstand or resort to petty partisanship, he [Rodino] retreated to his private quarters and he wept. (Paula Franzese, Seton Hall Law School)[11]

[8]Charles Rangel, "The Gentleman from New Jersey Representative Peter Rodino." http://rangel.house.gov/cr062005c.html
[9]Feltman.
[10]Paul S.Sarbanes. "Tribute to Congressman Peter W. Rodino, Jr." http://thomas.loc.gov/cgi-bin/query/R?r109:FLD001:S08484
[11]Paula A. Franzese, "Keep That Good Heart: The Life and Legacy of Congressman Peter W. Rodino." http://thomas.loc.gov/cgi-bin/query/R?r109:FLD001:S08484

RACHAEL DOMENICA RAY
Media Personality

"I was in the kitchen at an early age with my mother. In fact, I was in the kitchen watching my mother and learning about food even before I picked up a spoon! She'd have me on her hip while she stirred a pot on the stove and carried on a conversation. I saw how food plays an important role in our lives. In the kitchen, we can be creative,  *and if the turnout isn't what we wanted, it's no big deal—it's only food and it might still taste great. It's the idea that you are cooking together and sharing with someone the result of your hard work and creativity. Every time I cook, I'm making new memories and learning valuable skills that will last a lifetime.*[1]

"I've encouraged people not to be afraid of cooking and to give it a try. Especially kids! When I receive letters from people telling me that I've helped them in some way to overcome the fear of the kitchen, then I know I've done my job and made a difference."[2] (Rachael Ray)

Rachael Domenica Ray was born in Cape Cod, Massachusetts, in 1968. Her mother, Elsa Scuderi, was Italian American, and her father, James Ray, was French American. Food was a pivotal part in the family's livelihood. In fact, Rachael's maternal grandfather, Emmanuel Scuderi, and his family of 12 ate only what he had grown and cooked himself. Rachael's family owned several restaurants on Cape Cod before relocating to upstate New York, where her mother worked as the food supervisor for a restaurant chain.[3] Bouts of croup in early childhood left Rachael with her distinctive husky voice.[4]

---

[1] www.rachaelray.com/bio/php

[2] http://www.yum-o.org/message.php

[3] www.rachaelray.com/bio/php

[4] http://www.vanityfair.com/fame/features/2007/10/rachaelray200710?printable=true&curren

Food Is Never Far Away

In her early twenties, Rachael headed for New York City, where she landed a job at Macy's, first at the candy counter and then as manager of the fresh foods department. She credits her two years at Macy's for giving her an education in gourmet foods. From Macy's she helped open Agata & Valentina, the prestigious New York gourmet marketplace. She became store manager and buyer for A&V.

Tiring of city life, Ray returned to upstate New York, managing restaurants and pubs at the famed Sagamore Resort on Lake George. Her next stop was Albany, New York, where she became first the food buyer and then the chef for Cowan & Lobel, a large gourmet market.

As a way to increase grocery sales during the holidays, Ray began a series of cooking classes, promising to teach "30-Minute Mediterranean Meals." The classes turned out to be so popular, the CBS station in Albany-Schenectady, WRGB-TV, signed her on to do a weekly "30-Minute Meals" segment for the evening news. Nominated for two regional Emmys in its first year, the segment was a major success. A companion cookbook sold 10,000 copies locally during the holidays.

A Star—and a Franchise—Are Born

Next came lifestyle and travel segments as well as a long-term relationship with the Food Network. Ray hosted shows such as "Tasty Travels," "$40 A Day," and "Inside Dish." For "30 Minute Meals," Ray won a 2006 Daytime Emmy Award for Outstanding Service Show and a nomination for Outstanding Service Show Host.

There were bestselling series of cookbooks, including *30-Minute Meals, 30-Minute Meals 2, 30-Minute Meals: Get Togethers, Comfort Foods, Veggie Meals, The Open House Cookbook, Cooking 'Round the Clock Rachael Ray 30-Minute Meals, Cooking Rocks! Rachael Ray 30-Minute Meals for Kids, Rachael Ray Best Eats In Town on $40 A Day, Rachael Ray 30-Minute Get Real Meals, Rachael Ray 365: No Repeats A Year of Deliciously Different Dinners,* and *Express Lane Meals.*

Rachael the Editor

In 2005, Ray launched her own lifestyle magazine, *Every Day With Rachael Ray.* With great food at its heart, the full-size glossy magazine, for which Ray serves as editor-in-chief, covers much more than food. The magazine offers recipes as well as advice on food destinations and entertaining. Through the magazine, Ray takes readers around the country to meet people who love food—from top celebrities to authentic artisans to great home cooks.

In 2006, *Time* magazine named Ray one of the country's most influential people. In that same year, Ray ranked second, behind only Tom Hanks, in *Forbes* magazine's list of the Ten Most Trusted Celebrities.[5]

On September 18, 2006, the "Rachael Ray" show debuted on television, with Ray as host. In the hour-long daytime show, Ray shares secrets for fearless, can-do living and offers simple solutions to everyday problems. The show received seven daytime Emmy award nominations in its first year.

I Am Who I Am

With success often comes criticism. Some people criticize Ray's perkiness while others say she does not have the solid credentials of renowned chefs. Ray does not apologize for her effervescent personality. As for her credentials, she admits to being a "cook," not a "chef." And so much of her appeal to millions of people is the simple, down-to-earth approach she takes that makes people believe "I can do that."

Giving Back

Despite her crowded schedule, Ray uses her talents, resources, and celebrity status to help people eat better and healthier. For example, she highlights the issue by having as showguests youngsters who are struggling with weight but working hard to eat better and healthier. In 2006, she launched Yum-o!™, a nonprofit organization that empowers kids and their families to develop healthy relationships with food and cooking by teaching families to cook, by feeding hungry kids, and by funding cooking education and scholarships. Yum-o! partners in these endeavors with various nonprofit organizations.[6]

---

[5]http://www.vanityfair.com/fame/features/2007/10/rachaelray200710?printable=true&curren

[6]http://www.yum-o.org/cook_feed_fund.php

Share Our Strength. According to the United States Agriculture Department, 35 million Americans suffered from hunger in 2006. Found in all regions of the country, rural and urban, that number translates to 12.6 percent of all families and 13 million children—one in five.[7] As a core part of its Feed program, Yum-o! is partnering with Share Our Strength® (SOS) to raise money in support of its leading priority: ending childhood hunger in America. By offering ongoing, direct financial support and through Rachael's appearances in support of SOS, Yum-o! is helping reach out to at-risk kids and surround them with the nutritious food they need to learn, grow, and thrive.

Alliance for a Healthier Generation (a joint initiative of the William J. Clinton Foundation and the American Heart Association). Yum-o! collaborates with the Alliance for a Healthier Generation to empower families across America (where childhood obesity is a serious problem) to make healthy food choices by providing them with the tools and information they need to transform their eating habits. Such efforts will help kids live longer, healthier lives. Ray said: "A huge part of the obesity problem is that kids and their families are pressed for time and many don't know how to cook or assemble basic, healthy meals. . . . Parents from all walks of life and incomes have told me they are willing and eager to make better food choices for their families if given the right tools and know-how. I am absolutely thrilled to be working with the Alliance to make this happen."

The National Restaurant Association Educational Foundation. Yum-o! and NRAEF, the educational arm of the National Restaurant Association, have launched a scholarship initiative aimed at providing funds to high school students committed to pursuing a career in the restaurant and food service business.[8]

Success has not spoiled Rachael Ray. Instead it has given her the opportunity and potential to reach out and help so many. And she is doing just that.

---

[7] http://www.reuters.com/article/domestic/News/idUSN

[8] http://www.yum-o.org/partner.php. Other reference materials for Rachel Ray include http://www.popstarplus.com/celebrities_rachaelray.htm; "Rachael Ray's Yum-o! Organization Partners with the Alliance for a Healthier Generation to Improve How American Families Eat," Alliance for Healthier Generation Press Release, April 26, 2007; "Over 35 million Americans faced hunger in 2006": USDA; photo: www.rachaelray.com/bio/php

JOHN CIARDI
Poet, Teacher

As a young boy, John Ciardi moved with his family from the predominantly Italian North End of Boston to a heavily Irish section of Medford, Massachusetts. The transition was not without incident, even in church, with other boys and the priest, as Ciardi later recorded in one of his poems:

> *His nose well blown,*
> *he stood above us, outside the altar rail*
> *and worked the boys up to three last Green Cheers:*
> *"Where did Saint Patrick come from?"*
> *"Ireland!" the saved screamed.*
> *"And where did he bring his blessing?"*
> *Again: "Ireland!"*
> *"And where did your fathers come from?"*
> *Once again*
> *he got his chorus but he lost my soul.*
> *I heard a bellowing of lunatic treason:*
> *"FROM ITALY, BY GOD!"*
> *And didn't know*
> *I was the lunatic till he grabbed my ear*
> *and dragged me to the altar: "PRAY FOR YOUR SOUL!"*
> *But I'd be damned first.*[1]

John Ciardi was the fourth child and only son of Italian immigrant parents, Carminantonio and Concetta Ciardi. Carminantonio supported his family by going door-to-door collecting five- and ten-cent burial insurance premiums. When John was only three, his father was killed in an automo-

---

[1]Edward M. Cifelli, *Ciardi, John: A Biography* (Fayetteville: U of Arkansas P, 1997) 16.

bile accident. Concetta, who was illiterate in both Italian and English, had to rely on her skills as a seamstress, a second job in a factory, and the help of relatives to care for John and his three sisters. John helped out as he got older by taking menial jobs, such as selling produce for local merchants.

On his first day of school in Medford, John was teased for the Buster Brown outfit he was wearing and got into a fight. But his most disconcerting moment of that day came in the classroom when his teacher mispronounced his name. He later wrote of the incident in a poem called "A Knothole in Spent Time":

Omniscience had changed my name! I was John Sea-YARD-i
—and not even allowed to argue! What's a teacher
if she can't say a name right? . . . John Sea-YARD-i . . .
That was no sound of mine. I was John CHAR-di.

After high school, Ciardi attended Bates College, for which his three sisters helped pay the tuition. But not finding what he was looking for at Bates, Ciardi transferred to Tufts, where he did find his lifelong passion— poetry. Working under a young professor at Tufts, Ciardi began writing poetry seriously and sought out the harshest critics he could find. After graduating from Tufts, he went to University of Michigan for his MA, with the help of money that came with an award he had won in a writing competition. From there Ciardi went to the University of Kansas City, where he taught writing and literature.

Soon after World War II broke out, Ciardi enlisted and became a gunner on B-29 Superfortresses, and flew 20 missions over Japan. When an officer found out that Ciardi was a writer, he was taken out of the planes and put before a typewriter. His duty was to write merit citations and personalized letters of condolence to families of fallen comrades.

Following the war, Ciardi returned to Kansas City University to teach. One of his students wrote of him: "He seemed to crackle with vitality and for me, he made those classes come alive. You could tell he loved what he was doing, and he wanted you to love it as well."[2]

---

[2]Cifelli 99.

His Mission

Getting others to read, understand, and love poetry became Ciardi's mission. For too long, poetry had been the province of the "literary establishment"—the specialists, the academics. Ciardi made a conscious effort to reach the average reader.[3] Though he hoped to spread appreciation for poetry, he would not do so at the risk of lowering his very high standards. The good poet writes with discipline, Ciardi said. It is not enough to just pour out one's emotions, as so many contemporary poets were doing. The emotion has to be felt by the reader, and to convey such emotion the poet must work to shape the language. He wrote *How Does a Poem Mean?*, a textbook for novice readers still used in colleges and high schools today.

Ciardi taught for a number of years at Harvard and Rutgers, where he was a student favorite, despite the rigorous demands he made on them. One student wrote that Ciardi "managed to show those of us lucky enough to work under him that he did care very much about human beings."

Broadening the Audience

Ciardi traveled widely to give lectures, seminars, and workshops in poetry to a broad range of audiences—from college students to women's clubs to children. Ciardi carried his message to people the establishment would never reach, winning over groups such as fraternity brothers.

He often used "unconventional" media to convey his message. For example, he was poetry editor for and wrote a column in *Saturday Review* for many years. He was a regular commentator on National Public Radio, where he delivered a weekly series entitled "A Word in Your Ear," which is still available online. Ciardi's thoughts on poetry showed up in unlikely places, such as his article "Why Read Modern Poetry?" in an IBM publication. Ciardi appeared in a number of television programs focused on literature, and he became such a popular figure that he twice appeared as a guest on the *Tonight Show, with Johnny Carson*. Late in his career he published collections of word histories, again, not for the academics but for the average reader.

Perhaps because of his popularity, Ciardi's views on the racial strife in the United States in the 1960s became news. This comment encapsu-

---

[3] John Ciardi, http://www.poets.org/printpoet.php/prmPID/680.

lates his attitude: "We cannot survive as a nation in which nine-tenths of our citizens are automatically superior to the other tenth because of skin color and facial features."[4]

His Body of Work

While teaching and touring extensively, Ciardi managed to produce a large body of his own work. His poetry collections cover his family, the Italian American heritage and immigrant experience, his war experiences, the American dream, and a country preoccupied with material gain.[5] He wrote many of what he called "unimportant poems," which treated daily activities of ordinary people.

He also wrote several volumes of children's poetry, with titles such as *The Man Who Sang the Sillies,* in which wordplay and humor take an important role. Even in his children's poetry, however, Ciardi maintained his discipline and very high standards. His children's books received numerous awards from groups such as the Boys Clubs of America and the National Council of Teachers of English. One reviewer said of Ciardi: "Practically singlehandedly, he changed the whole character of American poetry for children.[6] Another wrote: "He altered the way we look at poetry for children, helping us see it as a fun-filled romp instead of a saccharine pill or a dose of propriety."[7]

Making the Divine Comedy *Accessible*

Perhaps his most significant single accomplishment was his translation of Dante's *Divine Comedy,* which was 16 years in the making. Having grown up with the Italian language, Ciardi felt that none of the then current translations of Dante's great work conveyed the sense of the original Italian. Ciardi used idiomatic language to bring to readers of English the power of the original.

---

[4]Cifelli 277.
[5]Enotes.com, "Ciardi, John," vol. 129.
[6]Cifelli 296.
[7]Cifelli 303.

One reviewer wrote of Ciardi's translation that his "style, moreover, was plain as much of the 'Inferno' is plain, dramatic where Dante is dramatic, with touches of vulgarity and grim humor to match those of the original, which are normally glossed over or unrecognized."[8] Another wrote: "Here is our Dante, Dante for the first time translated into virile, tense American verse."[9] Others must have agreed, as Ciardi's translation sold more than 60,000 copies in the first six months and some three million copies total.

One of Ciardi's sons—John—said of his father: "He grew up poor, the son of immigrant parents, but he went on to do what he loved and realize the American dream." Fortunately for generations of readers, John Ciardi also gave back.

---

[8]Cifelli 174.
[9]Cifelli 303.
photo: http://www.harvardsquarelibrary.org/poets/ciardi.php

GERALDINE A. FERRARO
Congresswoman, Vice Presidential Candidate

"Ladies and gentlemen of the convention: My name is Geraldine Ferraro. I stand before you to proclaim tonight: America is the land where dreams can come true for all of us. . . .

"I proudly accept your nomination for Vice President of the United States. . . .

"Tonight, the daughter of a woman whose highest goal was a future for her children talks to our nation's oldest party about a future for us all.

"Tonight, the daughter of working Americans tells all Americans that the future is within our reach—if we are willing to reach for it.

"Tonight, the daughter of an immigrant from Italy has been chosen to run for Vice President in the new land my father came to love.

"Our faith that we can shape a better future is what the American dream is all about. The promise of our country is that the rules are fair. If you work hard and play by the rules, you can earn your share of America's blessings."
(Geraldine A. Ferraro, Speech Accepting Nomination for Vice President)[1]

Geraldine A. Ferraro is the daughter of Dominick Ferraro, an immigrant from Italy, and Antonetta Ferraro, a first-generation Italian American. Tragedy struck the family when Dominick died at a young age. Geraldine was eight years old. Antonetta was determined to raise her family, which also included a son, on her own. She moved her family from Newburgh, New York, to a small apartment in the South Bronx, the neighborhood later portrayed for its harshness in the movie *Fort Apache*.

Working as a seamstress, Antonetta stressed the importance of education, even sending Geraldine to private school. Geraldine later wrote of her mother's saying: "Don't forget your name. *Ferro* means iron. You can

---

[1] http://www.infoplease.com/t/hist/ferraro-acceptance/

bend it, but you can't break it."[2] Later, when Geraldine was in college, an uncle chided Antonetta for sending her daughter to college. "She is pretty," he said. "She'll get married." "She's going to get an education," Antonetta insisted.

Geraldine worked two and sometime three jobs to help pay her way through college. And then she took a job teaching in public school while attending law school at night. Ferraro wrote: "I had to fight for whatever I wanted, to work and study my own way out of the South Bronx and take my mother with me."[3]

Making Her Mark

After marrying John Zaccaro, she stayed at home for 14 years to raise her three children. Then she made the difficult transition, returning to work full time in 1974 as an assistant district attorney in Queens County. She soon became chief of the Special Victims Bureau, handling all of the sex crimes in Queens, all referrals from family court on child abuse, and all violent crimes against senior citizens. But after four years, she felt she wanted to do more—to be in a better position to prevent such crimes. That meant shaping the legislation that was needed. That would mean running for Congress.

In a surprising upset, Ferraro won the election for Congress from New York City's Ninth District in 1978. This victory would be followed by two more, giving Ferraro three consecutive terms in Congress.

Immediately she set up a storefront Congressional office. She wanted her constituents to be able to walk in off the street and share their issues with her. She also made it a point to go out to elderly and disabled citizens who could not make it to her office.

A Warrior for Women

One of the recurring issues brought to her was discrimination against women. Ferraro didn't need to hear her constituents' stories—though she heard many—as she had experienced discrimination first hand. For example, after graduating from law school she interviewed with a number

---

[2]Geraldine A. Ferraro, with Linda Bird Francke, *Ferraro: My Story* (New York: Bantam Books, 1985) 17.
[3]Ferraro 18.

of firms. After the fifth interview with one firm she felt the job was hers. But the partner said, "We think you're terrific, but we're not hiring any women this year." Another instance was at the Queens DA's office, where Ferraro received a lower rate of pay than other bureau chiefs with similar responsibilities. Even when she was a public figure running for election to Congress she could not get a credit card in her own name. After three years in Congress, she could not get a VISA card from Citibank on the first time around.[4]

In Congress, she was an advocate for women's and human rights, working for the passage of the Equal Rights Amendment. It took time, but in 1983, Congresswoman Ferraro (she used her given name rather than her husband's in honor of her mother and father) sponsored and was instrumental in the passage of the Women's Economic Equity Act. Among other provisions, the Act ensured private pension equity for women and also sought greater job training and opportunities for displaced homemakers.[5]

Feisty and Smart

Establishing herself in Congress, Ferraro was called on to hold numerous positions in the Democratic Party. Among these was chairing the critical Platform Committee prior to the 1984 convention. Her success in setting party policy that was universally accepted had much to do with Walter Mondale's tapping her to be his running mate against incumbent President Ronald Reagan and Vice President George Bush.

The campaign was long, grueling, and, at times, dirty. Her opponents tried to attack Ferraro on a number of fronts, principally her being a woman, her husband's business dealings, and her Italian heritage. Through it all, Ferraro proved to be strong and persevering. She quickly developed a reputation for being feisty, and in time showed the voters that she was also intelligent and knowledgeable on the issues. In her only televised debate, when George Bush tried to demean her knowledge of foreign policy, she shot back: "Let me say first of all that I resent, Vice President Bush, your patronizing attitude that you have to teach me about foreign policy."[6]

---

[4]Ferraro 137.
[5]http://www.greatwomen.org/women.php?action=viewone&id=61
[6]Ferraro 260.

A Loss and a Gain

In the contest against a sitting president during peacetime when the economy was good, Mondale and Ferraro lost the election. But Ferraro's campaign made great gains for women in politics, erasing the negative stereotyping of women candidates. Ferraro reflected on the campaign and its impact:

> Yes, the 1984 campaign was dirty. Yes, the Republicans beat us. But was my run for the Vice Presidency worth it? Sure was. Regardless of what it cost us personally, the benefits of my candidacy to women, all women, eased the pain. From the moment of my nomination in San Francisco, my candidacy touched a nerve in the country.[7]

In 1992, Ferraro was narrowly defeated in the Democratic senate primary, as she was again in 1998. She served as a television commentator and a US Representative on the United Nations Human Rights Commission.[8] She was also a Teaching Fellow at the John F. Kennedy School of Government at Harvard University, and she was president of the International Institute for Women's Political Leadership.

Still Fighting the Good Fight

In 1998, Ferraro was diagnosed with multiple myeloma, a form of blood cancer that afflicts 50,000 Americans. She was given three years to live, yet in 2007 she told Jamie Gangel of *Today* that "I feel great." She was in remission and relying on maintenance medication, without having to undergo the side effects of traditional chemotherapy.

The medication is called Velcade, approved in 2004, and it is bringing the disease under control. Ferraro laments, however, that because of its high cost, more people cannot take advantage of it. She tries to inspire other cancer patients to keep fighting and she works to raise funds for research into cures.[9]

---

[7]Ferraro 318.
[8]http://print.infoplease.com/ce6/people/A0818528.html
[9]http://www.msnbc.msn.com/id/20527638
photo: Biographical Directory of the United States Congress

FRANCESCO "FRANK" MUSORRAFITI
Businessman

On September 11, 2001, Francesco "Frank" Musor-rafiti was planning to make the trip to lower Manhattan for a meeting. Planning the trip with his assistant, he assumed the car ride and then the short subway ride on the PATH train would get them to South Ferry Terminal at about 9:40 AM. The meetings of the USS Bulkely DDG-84 Commissioning Committee were known to be lengthy, as this committee was comprised of about 50 very enthusiastic members. Frank had an important client meeting scheduled for two o'clock back at Fort Monmouth in New Jersey. He would be cutting it too tight. So he asked for and received a postponement of the meeting. That fortuitous change in plans, of course, enabled Frank to avert being caught in the attack on the World Trade Center.

Frank's response: "Somebody was watching out for me."

In 1922, Vincenzo Musorrafiti left the small town of Podargoni in Reggio Calabria, Italy, and headed for New York. A year later, he married Antoinette Calarco, also from Calabria. They had three children—Giuseppe "Joseph," Damian "Diana," and Francesco "Frank." Self-educated, Vincenzo worked as a laborer and a stationary plant engineer for the New York Central Railroad. Later he became president of the Firemen and Oilers Local 92. After living in a couple of places in Manhattan, the family settled in East Harlem, when Frank was eight years old.

Surviving the Streets
"That's where I learned the facts of life," Frank recalls.

"It was a place where life on the streets was hard. There were plenty of turf battles, with lines often drawn according to national background. You had to form the right alliances and master survival strategies if you intended to live in that neighborhood. It is only because I had good, strong parents that I made it. There was no question that in our family you followed the rules. Both my mother and father insisted that we go to school and apply ourselves. If my mother hadn't been home every day when I got out of school, I could have gotten into some big trouble."

Besides the firm guidance of his parents, Frank points to a woodworking teacher at rough-and-tumble Patrick Henry Junior High School, which was 98 percent Black and Puerto Rican. "For whatever reason," Frank said, "this teacher took an interest in him and another boy, named Tony Spadara." The teacher pulled the two of them aside one day and said, "You two are going to Stuyvesant." That just happened to be one of the top three schools in New York City, where students were admitted only after passing a rigorous exam. "This was a teacher we respected," he said. "Had another teacher made that suggestion, I would have said 'thank you but no thanks,' and gone to the local public high school. Had I gone to the local high school, I might have wound up a 'hood,' like a lot of my classmates from Patrick Henry—if I lived through it."

In the Navy

After Frank graduated high school, his father asked him if he would like to attend the US Naval Academy. Frank's brother, Joseph, had been in the Navy during World War II, so Frank said Yes. Before applying to the Academy, however, Frank became a Seaman Recruit. This experience would not only give him some background but also put him in good standing for an appointment to the Academy, in case his Congressional appointment did not come through.

His parents put aside what little money they had to send Frank to a prep school to ready him for the entrance exam. Frank passed the exam on the second try and entered the Academy. As a plebe (a freshman) Frank had to make one drastic adjustment. He had to learn to take orders from many people at various levels of authority. "For a kid who never took orders from anyone but his father and mother, the Academy was tough. But I knew my parents had put up money to send me to prep school and I didn't want to embarrass them." Frank followed orders and in retrospect sees that experience as "good training." Besides learning discipline, Frank also learned teamwork. Frank graduated with his class, receiving a Bachelor of Science degree in Engineering. He then began his 20-year career in the Navy.

Frank served as a line officer, sailing on destroyers, amphibian craft, and an aircraft carrier for 11 years. "I loved the Navy and I loved being at sea," he said. Following up on his Academy education, the Navy sent Frank to US Naval Post Graduate School in Monterrey, California. There he received a degree in nuclear engineering. The main premise of this training was to enable him to plan nuclear missions to achieve their military objective with the least destructive force. For example, the right amount of force would be used to destroy a target without damaging areas around it. His graduation thesis was on the effects of radiation on the human body.

Intelligence Agencies

With this background in nuclear missiles, Frank was back at sea, conducting tests of weaponry and its effects on various vessels. He was then assigned to shore duty from 1968 to 1973. First he was assigned to the US Arms Control and Disarmament Agency. Having gained special clearances, he was then assigned to the Defense Intelligence Agency. These five years were a mixed blessing. As a line officer, he was on shore duty too long, hurting his chances of climbing in rank. The saving grace, however, was that his education and experiences in intelligence gave him the background to build Engineering & Professional Services (EPS), his company that today employs more than 600 people stationed in various parts of the world. Many of the EPS employees hold security clearances.

Still Serving His Country

In explaining his business, Frank says EPS supports our armed forces. The US Armed Services "outsource" jobs that can be done by someone else so that soldiers can focus on the business of soldiering. For example, when the United States had a considerable presence in Kosovo, EPS had 90 of its people there for five years, handling all communications operations and maintenance, working 12-hour shifts, seven days a week.

Other examples of its work include building a massive computer network for the Navy and manufacturing radios that enable military helicopters to locate downed pilots.

EPS has over 150 technical trainers who can write instructional programs from beginning to end to meet all the requirements of the US Army.

EPS has "platform trainers" who have taught over half a million troops to use various telecommunications systems. The company installs and repairs equipment in such places as Kuwait, Afghanistan, Saudi Arabia, and China. EPS has delivered infrastructure upgrades to 50 US Embassies and Consulates.

Commercial Endeavors

EPS is comprised of 10 separate divisions with core competencies in the areas of training, logistics support, program management, systems integration and engineering, telecommunications, physical security, information technology, structured cabling infrastructure solutions and design and maintenance of mission critical infrastructures. Not all of EPS's work is with the military. For example, the company has recently been awarded a major contract to provide a range of services needed in rebuilding the infrastructure for the subway system in Bucharest, Rumania.

EPS, together with WonderWorks Entertainment Group and the cities of Santa Marinella and Tolfa, Italy, is about to embark on a multi-billion dollar project—"Etruscan Theme Park." Located on 3,500 acres within the Lazio Region—about 30 miles from Rome—Etruscan Theme Park will be comprised of a number of elements. Besides an entertainment component, the Park will feature hotels, condominiums, homes, and golf courses. In addition to managing the project, EPS will install the entire infrastructure. This project will have an immediate effect on local employment levels, creating 6,000 construction jobs. Upon completion, the Park will fill 4,000 full-time positions.

Giving Back

Using his training and background, Frank has given back in a number of ways. When the Federal government planned to close down Fort Monmouth in New Jersey, Frank put EPS resources into the Patriots Alliance Inc., an all-volunteer, non-profit corporation whose mission was to support Fort Monmouth in its efforts to remain a viable entity. The company participated through fundraising, an awareness campaign, appearances before local groups, and research into all applicable areas.

When citizens wanted to bring the Battleship *New Jersey* from Bremerton, Washington, where it had been retired in 1999, back to its home state, Frank was chosen to head the "special team" of The Battleship's Commission. At his own expense, he traveled to Bremerton, to Washington DC, and to Panama in efforts to get permission for the ship to pass through the Panama Canal, expediting the battleship's transit from the West Coast to the East Coast. A plan was devised and submitted to the Panama Canal Commission, which rarely gave permission for a ship of the *New Jersey's* size to pass through the canal. But the team did win permission, and the ship was towed through the canal "with only one foot to spare on either side." For his efforts, Frank received the 2002 Monmouth-Ocean Development Council Silver Gull Award for Tourism.

Frank's office is adorned with plaques, citations, and other mementoes applauding him for his integrity and commitment to society. For example:

- For years, Frank served on the Board of Directors of the USO, bringing ideas on how this group could better serve the troops and keep morale high.
- He chaired the Commissioning Ceremonies of the *USS Bulkely* DDG-84 in New York City, after working diligently for that ship's commission.
- He serves as Trustee for the Battleship *New Jersey* (BB62). As a member of the Executive Committee, he is seeking ways to make this educational tool more available to the children of the state.
- In 2004 he was honored by the Monmouth Park Charity Ball Committee for his outstanding leadership and contribution to the community.
- Frank served on the board of Commissioners of Pilotage of the State of New Jersey, a body that ensures that foreign ships entering New Jersey ports meet all regulations, thereby safeguarding the state's ports and people.
- In 2004, Frank was named an Ernst & Young Entrepreneur of the Year finalist. This award is given to "entrepreneurial leaders and visionaries—men and women who create market-leading businesses, contribute to the strength of their communities and the economy, and help raise the bar of business excellence."
- In 2005, he received the *Italian Tribune's* prestigious Columbus

Award, given to Americans of Italian descent and recognizing their notable achievements.

- He received the Ellis Island Medal of Honor, which pays tribute to "remarkable Americans who exemplify outstanding qualities in both their personal and professional lives, while continuing to preserve the richness of their particular culture."

Frank Musorrafiti has never forgotten where he comes from, the people who helped him get where he is today, and the country that gave him the opportunity. As he says so often and so humbly, "Only in America."

Infomation contained here comes from personal interviews with Francesco Musorrafiti.
Photo: Frank Musorrafiti

JOSEPH VINCENT PATERNO
Coach, Teacher

Considered one of the best college football coaches of all time, Joe Paterno racked up record numbers of victories. More importantly, he spent more than 43 years developing character in young men at Penn State University. At a time when many college athletic programs are little more than sports factories, Paterno's reputation for putting the education of his charges above their football prowess ranks him among only a handful of coaches who achieved such great success on the field while insisting on performance in the classroom.

Over the years, Paterno received many offers to move on to coach teams at schools with bigger programs (and budgets) as well as in the professional ranks. He came close to leaving Penn State in 1972, when the New England Patriots organization of the National Football League offered Joe a financial package that amounted to about $1.4 million. For a family man earning $35,000 a year, this arrangement would have freed frugal Paterno from any and all financial worries, while giving him a prominent position at football's highest level. Besides offering a $200,000 home with a two-car garage, two cars, and a starting salary of $200,000 a year, the Patriots were willing to give Paterno total control of the football operation as well as part ownership of the team. Reluctant to leave Penn State, Paterno kept coming up with requests for additional perks, so he would have reason to reject the offer. But the Patriots met each outrageous demand. Paterno accepted the offer.

Then he rejected it. At a press conference he explained his acceptance and his reversal. "I realized that I was merely flattered by the amount of money, and I got back to what I really wanted to do. I realized that I wouldn't be happy just being a football coach in which winning and losing is everything."[1]

---

[1]Michael O'Brien, *No Ordinary Joe* (Nashville, TN: Rutledge Hill P, 1998) 93. Photo appears courtesy of Penn State University's Department of Public Information. http://live.psu.edu/album/162

A fierce competitor who never liked to lose, Joe Paterno dedicated his life to something more than winning games—building character.

Joseph Vincent Paterno was born on December 21, 1926, the first child of Angelo and Florence Paterno, in Brooklyn, New York. Both parents were first-generation Italian Americans. After high school, Florence worked for the telephone company. Angelo dropped out of high school to serve under General John Pershing in the United States Army, fighting in campaigns in Mexico and World War I. After the service, he took a clerical job in the appellate division of the New York Supreme Court. In the evenings, Angelo completed high school, college, and law school. The value he placed on education was not lost on his son, Joe. In his autobiography, Joe wrote:

When, as a little kid, you keep hearing of how your father finished high school at night, and then you see him come home late every night from college classes, and then at the age of 15 you see all your uncles and aunts and cousins and neighbors celebrate because your father passed the bar exam, you get the feeling that education is really important.

Besides stressing the importance of education, Angelo taught Joe to put sports in perspective. After a game, the first thing Angelo asked was not, "Did you win?" but "Did you have fun?"

From his mother Joe acquired drive, intensity, and the pursuit of perfection. She always expected Joe to be at the top. "If we had a classroom spelling bee," Joe recalled, "I was expected to win it."

Though the Paternos had acclimated well to the American way, the family was not exempt from ethnic prejudice. When a young Joe complained that someone called him a "wop," his mother sat him down and recited the accomplishments of great Italians such as Michaelangelo, DaVinci, Garibaldi, Columbus, and Toscanini.[2]

Books and Education

Growing up, Joe was a Cub Scout, a Boy Scout, and an avid reader of *The Leatherstocking Tales,* Tom Swift, the Hardy Boys, and others. When

---

[2]O'Brien, 3–12.

Joe was a junior at Brooklyn Prep, he was taken under the wing of a Mr. Thomas Bermingham, who later became a Jesuit priest. Mr. Bermingham was impressed by Joe's love of books and the many fine authors Joe had read on his own. Joe was equally impressed by his young teacher, who offered to guide him in reading the classics and other works well beyond the scope of the curriculum. They met afternoons to discuss works such as Virgil's *Aeneid,* which Joe read in its original Latin. Joe learned from his mentor that it's "not how much we do but the excellence of what we do."[3] That principle guided him throughout his life.

Though Paterno played both basketball and football in high school—and loved and excelled in both—he knew that his primary responsibility was to get an education. He realized his parents were making great sacrifices to send him to this fine Jesuit school, and Joe was determined to make the most of it.

To help pay his way through high school, Joe worked every summer—as a baggage checker at Penn Station, a mail clerk, a camp counselor, and an usher at Ebbets Field in Brooklyn, where the Dodgers played. But paying for college called for a lot more than he and his family could muster. Paterno was offered a few partial scholarships for basketball and football, when a booster from Brown University offered to pay Joe's tuition to that Ivy League school in Providence, Rhode Island. That type of arrangement later became forbidden but at the time was perfectly legal. But before Paterno could enroll, he was drafted by the US Army and served in Korea as a radio operator. Released in August of 1946, he was able to get to Brown in time for the fall semester and football season.

A Thinking Quarterback

Paterno played quarterback and defensive back at Brown. After seeing him in a win over Harvard, one sportswriter for a New York newspaper wrote: "Paterno, the Brown quarterback, can't run. He can't pass. All he can do is think—and win."[4]

---

[3]O'Brien 22.
[4]O'Brien 31.

Life was good. Paterno was playing college football and enjoying it. He was enjoying even more, however, his exposure to things academic—the world of art, history, literature, music, politics. There was some tension when Paterno walked out on a fraternity that would not accept a student because he was a Jew. But overall Paterno took from Brown just about all a young man could take from a university.

Upon graduation, the plan was for him to attend law school, as his father always dreamed of Joe's becoming a lawyer. But fate stepped in. His football coach at Brown, Charles "Rip" Engle, had taken a job as head football coach at Penn State University. He asked Paterno to be his assistant, because he knew Engle's wing-T system. Paterno agreed, but for only one year. His father was not happy delaying law school, but would not stop Joe. His mother's response was something like, "You have to go to college to be a coach?"

Coach Paterno

After arriving at Penn State in 1950, Paterno would remain assistant coach until Engle retired in 1965. The president of the college at the time was Milton Eisenhower, brother of the famed World War II general and later US President. The college president saw a coach's role as one of teacher. He suggested that coaches mingle with teaching faculty and attend staff meetings. He set strict academic standards and wanted coaches to see to it that their athletes met those standards.

That was fine with both Coach Engle and Assistant Coach Paterno, who carried those ideals even further. Football players learned fast that at PSU classes were mandatory. If a player had a late afternoon class, the player was to attend that class and show up for practice afterwards. On home game days—Saturdays—if a player had a class scheduled, he was to attend that class before suiting up. Early on and throughout his career, Paterno kept reminding his players that they were in college to get an education and that sports came second.

For a good many years Paterno supervised a study hall for football players in the library. It was there he met a librarian, Sue Pohland, who would become his wife.

Coach Paterno came to love the atmosphere of PSU, taking advantage of its opportunities to attend concerts and lectures on campus and discuss things other than football with various faculty members. After 16 years as an assistant, Paterno was named head football coach at PSU.

The Grand Experiment

In Paterno's first year as head coach, the team turned in a record of five wins and five losses. "A good assistant," some critics said, "but not a head coach." Some PSU fans put it more strongly than that—they sent hate mail to Paterno's home.

Nevertheless, in 1967, Paterno installed "the Grand Experiment." It meant that, for one thing, there would be no football dormitory exclusively for the players. "He would jump down your throat in a second about your poor grades," Don Bailey, a former player recalled. One writer reported it as Paterno's ambition to make Penn State a perennial national football power but the way he would go about it would be unusual. The "screwy thing" about it, the writer said, was there would be "no under-the-table recruiting. No promises of medical school or Cadillacs. No redshirting or lowering of admission standards for athletes."

A professor once came to Paterno about a problem one of the football players was having, namely cutting the professor's class.

"Did you speak to him about it?" Paterno asked.

"I did, but I'm not going to speak to him again."

"Good," Paterno said. "If he cuts anymore, flunk him."

"What if he's your quarterback?"

"I don't care. If he gets by with cutting your class, he'll ruin my locker room. He'll tell everybody. The first thing you know, everybody will be thinking that is okay. I don't want to know who he is. Just flunk him."

This is not to suggest that Paterno was an elitist, unwilling to help kids overcome their backgrounds. Bob White was a sensational high school defensive tackle that many colleges, including PSU, wanted. But Paterno questioned the boy's ability to make it in the classroom. He had never read a whole book. Paterno offered him a trial. If he'd spend the summer getting extra tutoring in English from Mrs. Paterno, the coach would accept him. Bob White agreed, read the dozen books assigned, and wrote a paper on each. He was accepted, played football, struggled in the classroom but graduated with his class.

As Paterno put it: "We want our players to enjoy football. We want them to enjoy college. We want them to learn about art and literature and music and all the other things the college has to offer."[5] Because of his unique relationship to the academic faculty, coach Paterno was made a full professor at PSU, something rare among sports coaches.

Undefeated

On the football field, it did not take long for the Paterno formula to pay dividends. In 1968, Penn State went through the regular season undefeated. In 1969 and in 1973, the Nittany Lions again ran through the season without a loss. The image of Paterno in his thick-framed eyeglasses and rolled up pants over tennis shoes graced magazine covers and TV screens across the country.

A former player, place-kicker Matt Bahr, summed up his impression of Paterno this way: "He wants you to achieve more than you believe yourself capable of, which then prompts you on to greater heights. You feel like what you do is never quite good enough, [but] that's what a coach is for—to make you excel. Today, looking from the outside in, I realize why he did what he did."[6]

In his career of 42 years (and counting) as head coach, Paterno's teams have won 373 games (as of this writing) while losing just 124. He has more wins in bowl games than any other coach. His teams have won the national championship twice and have ranked among the top 10 in the nation 21 times. Paterno was named coach of the year at least five times by various organizations.

Perhaps the most important statistic to Paterno is in his players' graduation rate. Year after year PSU football players are among the highest in graduation rate, most recently exceeding the national average by 19 percentage points. Paterno has produced 19 first-team Academic All-Americans, 10 Hall of Fame Scholar Athletes, and 15 NCAA Postgraduate Scholarship winners.[7]

---

[5]O'Brien 75.
[6]O'Brien 188.
[7]O'Brien 204.

Giving Back

Besides devoting his life to the betterment of his players, Paterno has contributed considerable time, talent, and treasure to many worthy causes and charitable institutions. He has given talks for the benefit of the Boy Scouts, served a one-year term as state chairman of the American Cancer Society, worked on the national sports committee of the Multiple Sclerosis Foundation, and was appointed to Pennsylvania's Citizens' Committee on Basic Education. He also assisted on a variety of local projects in State College, Pennsylvania.

In addition, Joe and Mrs. Paterno have worked arduously to continually improve Penn State University. "I'd like to see Penn State number one in everything," he often said. Using his energy and his celebrity, Paterno became a leading fundraiser for the university, helping to raise $20 million for a new athletic arena.

With their gift of $170,000, the Paternos started the Paterno Libraries Endowment. At one point in 1987, Paterno was delivering a PSU fundraiser speech on average of once a week. Ultimately $352 million was raised for the Pattee Library expansion. In recognition of the Paternos' efforts, the school trustees named the addition the Paterno Library. In 1998, the Paternos donated $3.5 million toward new teaching positions, scholarships, a new interfaith spiritual center, and a sports hall of fame.

Just as his work with young people continues, so do Joe Paterno's efforts in giving back. Here are some of Joe Paterno's coaching and teaching principles:

- Coaches should not neglect the teaching aspects of their vocation. "I am supposed to be developing certain character qualities and teaching the young people who come under my influence some values in life."[8]
- "Don't baby the star. I'm tougher on the best player on the practice field than I am on anybody else."[9]

---

[8]O'Brien 141.
[9]O'Brien 180.

- No "hot dogs' on the team. Players who dance in the endzone after a touchdown ridicule the opponent.[10]

- Following a game that his team won after trailing at halftime, Joe said: "I don't want you to remember how you feel right now. . . . But I want you to remember how you felt when you were down 14–0 . . . and you were about to have your face put in the mud. . . . Remember how you kept your poise and held hands and pulled it out. Those are the things to remember, because you are going to be down, 14–0, a lot of times in your life."[11]

- "I hope they're not going to judge me on how many games I won or lost. . . . I hope they judge me on some other things, the impact we've had on people's lives. Some have been good, and, obviously, some have not been so good. But I hope the overall picture is that we have done some good for people."[12]

---

[10]O'Brien 180.

[11]O'Brien 184.

[12]O'Brien 303. Additional sources of information for this chapter are:
http://pabook.libraries.psu.edu/palitma[/bios/Paterno_Joseph_Vincent.html
http://www.nytimes.com/2007/09/06/sports/ncaafootball/06paterno.html

ARMANDO "ACE" ALAGNA
White House Photographer, Publisher

When Italy's worst-ever earthquake killed more than 550 people in northern Italy and left 80,000 homeless, Armando "Ace" Alagna moved swiftly to action. As publisher of the Italian Tribune, *an Italian American newspaper based in northern New Jersey, he announced to his readers and others the creation of the Italian Tribune News Earthquake Relief Fund. People wanted to help: they just needed a conduit to channel their donations. The Fund collected more than $1 million, and soon a Children's Day Care Center was under construction; Alagna was there to dedicate the building.*

Four years later, disaster struck again, this time in the Irpinia region in southern Italy. The quake killed 2,914 people, injured more than 10,000, and left 300,000 homeless. Once again, Alagna called out for help and got an overwhelming response. Not only did the Fund send aid to Italy, but when Alagna heard of a medicine shortage in Poland, he used the contacts he had made as a member of the White House Press Corps to cut through miles of red tape and had $800,000 worth of medicine and other supplies sent to Poland. Pope John Paul II granted Alagna a special private audience to thank him on behalf of Poland, the pope's homeland.

Armando's father, Mario Alagna, was a stonemason in Marsala, Sicily. He married Marianne Barbieri, who had grown up in Limbati, Calabria. The young couple left Italy and came to America in 1900, settling in Newark, New Jersey. Armando was born to them in 1925.

Capturing History

As a young man, Armando "Ace" Alagna became interested in photography. At first he photographed children, brides, and families. Soon he matched his photographic skills with his artistic temperament to gain a national reputation. While still a relatively young man, he was named a member of the White House Press Corps. Over the course of more than 20 years he was assigned to US Presidents Harry S. Truman, Dwight D. Eisenhower, John F. Kennedy, Lyndon B. Johnson, and Richard M. Nixon.

His proudest moment came when President Lyndon Johnson assigned Alagna to photograph the historic signing of the Immigration Bill on Liberty Island. Ace envisioned his father coming through this hallowed place years before to create opportunity and freedom for his family.

Rebuilding the Italian Tribune

In 1968, rather than see the voice of the struggling *Italian Tribune* go silent, Alagna bought the newspaper, one of the few publications catering to the Italian American community. He brought new life to the paper and lifted it to a new level of public penetration in its capacity as a molder of public opinion. Today it ranks as one of the country's leading Italian American publications, carrying on Alagna's dedication to the propagation of Italian American culture.

Celebrating His Heritage

Alagna and the *Italian Tribune* have served the Italian American community and society at large in many ways. He played a role in the naming of Columbus Day as a national holiday. He revived the Newark Columbus Day parade and served as its executive director for 30 years. He brought A-list celebrities, such as Joe DiMaggio, Bob Hope, Tony Bennett, Tommy LaSorda, and Connie Francis, as well as millions of dollars, to a city in dire need of an economic and social boost.

In 1988, Alagna was personally asked by the White House to host a Columbus Day celebration in New Jersey for President Ronald Reagan. Thousands came to see Alagna bestow the Columbus Bronze Award on the President.

His Help Saw No Boundaries

Alagna sought to help where and when help was needed. He did not limit his assistance to Italian Americans. For such efforts he received the National Boys Clubs Bronze Keystone Award, the Veterans of Foreign Wars Award, and the 1998 Ellis Island Medal of Honor. He was named commissioner of the Bi-Centennial Committee in 1976 and was on the Gubernatorial Inaugural Commission in New Jersey.

He opened many doors and fittingly was presented with the Key to the City of Newark, Atlantic City, and Hoboken in New Jersey, as well as Philadelphia and New Orleans. He was similarly honored with Keys to the City of Naples and Rome in Italy. Thanks to his long relationship with Walt Disney Studios, Alagna was named Grand Marshall for the opening of EPCOT Center in Orlando, Florida. He was named Knight of Malta, the highest honor bestowed on a lay person by the Catholic Church. And he was the first Italian American to receive the State of Israel Award for his contributions to the brotherhood of nationalities.

Moving Pictures

Alagna was a member of the Screen Actors Guild of America, the Guild of Italian American Actors, and the American Film Institute. He appeared in many major motion pictures and produced several documentaries about Italy.

When Alagna died, his funeral was held in St. Lucy's Church in Newark, a church his father had helped to build decades before. In a different way, Ace, too, was a builder.[1]

---

[1] Information here comes from Marion Alagna Fortunato's notes.
photo: Marion Alagna Fortunato

MOTHER FRANCES XAVIER CABRINI
Humanitarian

*In the late 1800s and early 1900s, when countless im-
migrants made their way to American shores, many were
in for a rude awakening. Not only were the streets not
paved with gold, but they were often infested with crime,
squalor, disease, and despair. Work was hard to come by,
as the immigrants didn't know the language, and they
could not negotiate the system. There was no organiza-
tional structure to help these foreigners adjust and fit in.
Fortunately, however, there were individuals who stepped
up to help. One such individual was Sister Frances Xavier
Cabrini, later known as Mother Cabrini, the first naturalized Italian American to be named a saint.*

Born Maria Francesca Cabrini in the Lombardy region of Italy on July
15, 1850, Maria was one of 13 children, only four of whom survived. Maria
was a small, sickly child who helped her parents work their farm. She applied a number of times to enter religious orders but was turned down
because of her poor health. Her fortunes changed when she was asked to
teach at a girls' school nearby, and later work at an orphanage. Being successful there, she was asked by the local bishop to found an order of nuns
who would do missionary work. Maria founded the Missionary Sisters of
the Sacred Heart of Jesus in November of 1880.

Maria took the name Sister Frances Xavier Cabrini because she hoped
to do missionary work in China, like the renowned Jesuit, Francis Xavier.
Pope Leo XIII, however, had a different idea. He asked then Mother Cabrini
to take her small community (six) of missionaries to the United States to
tend to the needs of poor, struggling immigrants, many of whom were
Catholic and Italian.

No Welcome Mat

The greeting she and her sisters received in New York City was typical of what many immigrants would find in the New World. The lodgings she had been promised did not exist. Mother Cabrini and her six sisters spent their first night in a tenement flat that was so overridden with vermin that they did not dare close their eyes the entire night. When Mother Cabrini went to see Bishop Corrigan, who was to support her mission, he provided a temporary place for the nuns to stay but backed off on the support he had promised. He would help fund a school but not the orphanage included in the original agreement.

But Mother Cabrini would not be put off that easily. Besides opening a school, she persisted in working to develop the orphanage. She was told that she would have to finance the venture herself, and could solicit funds from Italians only, who were struggling to keep a roof over their own heads. In time, though, Mother Cabrini won over the bishop, and he lifted that restriction. Soon she had the funding and opened an orphanage in West Park on the Hudson River.

To address the clear need for health care, Mother Cabrini took $250 in donations, bought 10 metal bed frames, and, in 1892, founded Columbus Hospital in two small tenement houses in lower Manhattan. Within two years, the hospital moved to its location on 19th Street in Gramercy Park and continued to expand its services to meet growing health care needs. In the early 1970s, Columbus Hospital merged with the Italian Hospital and changed its name to Cabrini Medical Center.[1]

Meeting Educational and Spiritual Needs

In 1899, Mother Cabrini founded the first bi-lingual school in New York specifically to advance the education of children of Italian immigrants. In her dealings with the Italian immigrants, Mother Cabrini brought a voice they understood and welcomed, as Italian-speaking clergy

---

[1]http://www.cabrininy.org/history.html

in New York were rare. While she catered to their worldly needs, she also brought to them a spirituality that was just as nourishing. They realized that God had not forgotten them.[2]

Mother Cabrini founded schools for immigrant families in Chicago, Scranton, and Newark, New Jersey.[3] To help fund these schools, Mother Cabrini High School was founded. This school opened as a "residential school for young ladies." It catered to wealthy immigrants who could afford tuition, some of which was redistributed to support the poorer schools. Mother Cabrini High School, which became a source of many vocations, still exists today at Fort Washington Avenue in New York as an institution dedicated to secondary education of young women.[4]

Mother Cabrini brought her high level of care, tenacity, and business acumen to help Italian immigrants in New Orleans and Seattle. In Colorado, she worked with immigrant miners. Many died in those mines, and Mother Cabrini helped their survivors, building a school and an orphanage.[5] She set up an orphanage in Passaic, New Jersey, and she converted a hotel in Chicago into Columbus Hospital. It was there that she died on December 22, 1917.

The Saint

In 1946, Pope Pius XII canonized Frances Xavier Cabrini a saint, the first naturalized United States citizen to receive this honor. Her canonization was a fitting tribute to this humble woman who devoted her life to helping new Americans. She founded 67 schools, hospitals, and orphanages in all, bringing solace and compassion to so many of various nationalities.

---

[2]http://education.csm.edu/students/tfascianella/st_frances_carbini.htm: 4.
[3]http://education.csm.edu/students/tfascianella/st_frances_carbini.htm: 6.
[4]http://www.cabrinihs.com/
[5]http://www.cabrinihs.com/
photo: http://www.saintisidore.org/religious-info/st-cabrini.htm

GUNNERY SERGEANT JOHN BASILONE
Military Service

The mission was to defend the narrow pass leading to the Henderson Airfield on Guadalcanal, Solomon Islands, in the Pacific. Because it was such a strategic facility, the Japanese threw their best troops in great numbers to try to win it over. For two days, 'C" Company, 1ˢᵗ Battalion, 7ᵗʰ Regiment, 1st Marine Division, was just as determined the Japanese would not take it. One of those Marines was Gunnery Sergeant John Basilone.

Born in 1916, in Buffalo, New York, one of 10 children of Salvatore and Dora Basilone, John was raised and educated in Raritan, New Jersey. While still a teenager, he developed a reputation as an up-and-coming light-heavyweight boxer, but at age 18 he decided to do his fighting for the United States Army. Soon after his enlistment, he was assigned to the Philippines, where he picked up the nickname "Manila John." Honorably discharged in 1937, he returned to Raritan. But anticipating his country's entry into the war raging in Europe, Basilone enlisted in the United States Marine Corps in July 1940.

The Biggest Battle of His Life

On October 24 and 25, 1942, Basilone found himself on Guadalcanal in the biggest battle of his life—to that point. In charge of two sections of heavy machine guns guarding the narrow pass leading to the airfield, Basilone saw that he and his gunners were vastly outnumbered.[1]

A Japanese wave knocked out the guns on Basilone's left. He lifted a machine gun and its tripod—about 90 pounds—and raced to the silenced

---

[1] http://thomas.loc.gov/cgi-bin/query/C?c108:./temp/~c1081FnQwk

gun pit and started firing. As Japanese fired mortar shells at him and charged him from the front, others slipped around to attack him from the rear. He held off the latter with his pistol. Short of ammunition, he ignored a stream of bullets to run 200 yards for more shells for himself and his depleted section. He fired so much his hands blistered. In the light of dawn, he and his buddies counted 38 Japanese dead. The Marines had held the line.

Serving in Whatever Way He Could

For his role in this defense of Henderson Airfield, Basilone was awarded the Congressional Medal of Honor; he was the first recipient of this award in World War II. The citation spoke, in part, of Basilone's "extraordinary heroism and conspicuous gallantry in action."[2]

The Government brought him stateside and sent him on tour to raise money for the war effort. He elicited pledges totaling more than $1.4 million dollars. His picture was splashed on the cover of *Life* magazine. The USMC offered to make him an officer and give him a job in Washington, DC. Basilone's response was: "I ain't no officer, and I ain't no museum piece. I belong back with my outfit."

The Battle of Iwo Jima

Back with the troops at Camp Pendleton, Basilone married Lena Riggi, also a USMC Sergeant. But their time together was short. On February 19, 1945, Basilone was at Iwo Jima, in another legendary bloody battle. Basilone's platoon was pinned to the sand by enemy gunfire, until he stood up and yelled "Get off the beach. Move out!" His men moved. Soon after, an enemy mortar round exploded. An hour and a half later, Basilone was dead. The Marines took Iwo Jima, and a few months later, Japan surrendered, ending the war.

---

[2]http://en.wikipedia.org/wiki/John_Basilone

[3]http://www.arlingtoncemetery.net/johnbasi.htm

photo: U.S. Naval Historical Center

http://www.history.navy.mil/photos/pers/uspers-b/j-basiln.htm

Sergeant Basilone's remains were later reinterred in Arlington National Cemetery. Posthumously, he was awarded the Navy Cross and the Purple Heart. He was the only enlisted Marine in World War II to have been awarded the three prestigious medals—Medal of Honor, Navy Cross, and Purple Heart.

Honors and Awards
- Congressional Medal of Honor
- Navy Cross
- Purple Heart
- Burial at Arlington National Cemetery
- *USS Basilone* (DD-824), Navy Destroyer, commissioned in 1949 in his name
- A section of US Interstate 5 in California named the "John Basilone Memorial Highway"
- "Basilone Field," football field at Bridgewater-Raritan High School
- A plaque at the US Navy Memorial in Washington, DC

Ella T. Grasso
Congresswoman, Governor

On Sunday, February 5, 1978, weather forecasters were predicting a major snowstorm for the Northeast. Their prediction became reality for the state of Connecticut on Monday when almost two feet of snow fell, paralyzing the state for days. Sustained winds of more than 35 miles per hour caused snowdrifts over ten feet high. The National Weather Service later classified the storm a blizzard. Governor Ella T. Grasso declared all of Connecticut in a State of Emergency. She personally directed emergency operations, kept the public informed, and even shoveled snow. She stayed at the State Armory around the clock. She forbade travel on all state roads. She ordered the National Guard in to maintain order and assist as needed. She demanded assistance from Washington, and President Carter named Connecticut a disaster area and eligible for emergency aid. She flew to stricken areas all over the state, offering hope and promises of aid. Flying over an open field, she saw the words "HELP ELLA" stomped into the snow. And help she did, earning her the gratitude, admiration, and respect of the people of the state, as well as the affectionate nickname "Mother Ella."[1]

Governor Ella T. Grasso embodied the American dream. More precisely, her parents dreamed the dream and Ella lived it.

James Tambussi came to America in 1904. Two years later, Maria Oliva arrived in the United States. Both came from Genoa, Italy, and settled in Windsor Locks, a small industrial town north of Hartford. James worked in mills and factories, and Maria worked as an assembler in an electric motor shop. Later, James opened a bakery with his brother, working 12

---

[1]Ella Giovanno Oliva (Tambussi) Grasso, Governor of Connecticut, 1975–1980. Connecticut State Library. http://www.cslib.org/gov/grassoe.htm

hours a day. In 1911, James and Maria were married and settled in Windsor Locks, in a neighborhood of mostly immigrants, many of whom were relatives and friends from the "old country."

On May 10, 1919, Ella Giovanna Oliva Tambussi was born. Maria fed her daughter a steady diet of books, magazines, and whatever kind of reading material she could find. Both parents stressed the importance of hard work and education. Ella attended private grammar school, St. Mary's, in Windsor Locks. Though a scholarship enabled her to attend the prestigious Chaffee School in Windsor for her high school education, Ella's parents had to scrape up money for transportation, books, and meals. The same was true when she went to Mount Holyoke College.

Impact of Schooling

At each level of schooling, Ella made the most of her opportunity and was influenced in ways that shaped her career. At St. Mary's, she was taken under the wing of Sister De Chantal, whom Ella would later call "the most remarkable woman I've ever met." She recalled that Sister De Chantal would tell "all the little kids that each of them had a very special gift and they had a special opportunity and there was one thing they could do better than anybody and they had an obligation to develop that quality." So, added Ella, "that became part of my thinking."[2]

The Chaffee School was quite different from anything Ella had known to that point in her life. Chaffee was a private prep school for girls destined to go on to exclusive private colleges. Most of its students came from wealthy and prominent families. Despite coming from a very different background, Ella did extremely well academically as well as in activities such as the drama club and a model League of Nations. No doubt, she helped pave the way for other children of immigrant and working class families to attend schools such as Chaffee.

Nurturing an Interest in the Working Class

After graduating from Chaffee, Ella attended Mount Holyoke College in Massachusetts. Ella was among a select group of women in an experi-

---

[2]Jon E. Purmont, "The Education of Ella Grasso," http://www.hogriver.org/issues/v02n04/ella_grasso.htm

mental "two-unit plan" in which Ella concentrated on two areas of study—economics and history. Here Ella was strongly influenced by Professor Amy Hewes, a teacher who had an active commitment to public service and advocated reforms in the workplace, particularly regarding women and children. As part of her course work, Ella visited factories, met managers, and attended trade union meetings with workers. Ella's senior honors thesis was entitled "Workmen's Compensation in the United States," and her master's thesis was on the history of the Knights of Labor. This early interest in the working class stayed with Ella throughout her career.

It was from Holyoke that Ella moved into the world of politics, believing "in a very real sense of a relationship between politics and the lives of people—that what happens to us was affected by government and I wanted to be a part of that government."

Public Servant

After graduation, Ella worked as an Interviewer for Connecticut's State Employment Service and then as Assistant Director of Research in the War Department Manpower Commission in Hartford. She had married Thomas Grasso, a schoolteacher in 1942, and in 1946, Ella became a fulltime homemaker and mother to her two children, Susanne and James.

It was six years later that Ella returned to work outside the home when she was elected state representative from Windsor Locks. That marked the beginning of her 28-year career in elected office, during which time she never lost an election. She quickly attracted the attention of the Democratic Party leaders. She served as Secretary of the State of Connecticut from 1958 to 1970. She was credited with turning that position into an "activist office,"[3] opening doors to any citizen seeking help. As Connecticut's Secretary of State, she devoted a great deal of attention to mental hospital reform, day care, and civil rights. One of her former employees, Kathy Johnson, said of Ella: "She ran an extremely tight ship. When you were in the office there was no play time. There was never any political

---

[3]Sen. Chris Dodd, "Statement of Senator Chris Dodd on the 25th Anniversary of Governor EllaGrasso's Inauguration,"
http://dodd.sentate.gov/index.php?q=node/3270/print&pr=press/Releases/00/0110b.htm

campaigning conducted during office hours. She's been super honest, Mrs. Clean."[4]

In 1970, Grasso was elected Congresswoman from the Sixth Congressional District, and was reelected in 1972. Senator Chris Dodd referred to Grasso's office as a "people's lobby."[5] To make herself accessible to her Connecticut constituents, Grasso installed a 24-hour-toll-free telephone line, dubbed the "Ella-Phone." She explained: "It's my way of bringing government closer to the people and the people closer to the government."[6]

Serving on Education and Labor and Veterans' Affairs Committees, Grasso fought to create and protect jobs and serve those who had served the nation. She also worked on and influenced the National Cooley's Anemia Control Act of 1972, assisting victims of this disease. But thinking she could do more for more people at the state level, Grasso left Washington and ran for state governor. In 1974, she was elected Governor of Connecticut, the first woman to be elected state governor in her own right, that is, without assuming the office formerly held by her husband.

Enduring Some Hard Times

Upon assuming office as governor in 1975, Grasso set the tone for her administration quickly. She worked long and hard and expected others to do the same. She stayed close to the people by visiting factories and housing complexes to learn about conditions, so she could move to improve them.[7]

But the 1970s were not good years for most state governors, and Grasso was no exception. The economy was weak, interest rates were high, and a gasoline shortage resulted in long lines at service stations and short tempers among citizens. On top of all that, Grasso inherited a $70 million debt from the previous administration. Reflecting the need to economize,

---

[4]"Ella Grasso: first woman elected state Governor,"
http://www.essortment.com/ellagrasso_rfxy.htm
[5]Purmont, http://www.hogriver.org/issues/v02n04/ella_grasso.htm
[6]"Ella Grasso: first woman elected state Governor,"
http://www.essortment.com/ellagrasso_rfxy.htm
[7]"Ella Grasso: first woman elected state Governor,"
http://www.essortment.com/ellagrasso_rfxy.htm

she returned to the state treasury a $7,000.00 raise she could not legally refuse.[8]

Without funding, Grasso could not deliver on a number of the social programs she had promised in her campaign. But she did manage to get legislation passed to help consumers, and the Freedom of Information Act became law. Even as the budget deficit continued to grow, Grasso resisted pressures to implement a state sales tax. But hard times needed tough decisions, decisions that often were not popular. She called a special session of the legislature and proposed tapping into the Veterans' Fund and requiring state employees to work more hours for the same pay. When the General Assembly rejected both proposals, Grasso laid off 505 state employees—just days before Christmas.[9] Needless to say, many people were unhappy with her.

Matters improved somewhat in 1976. Connecticut introduced a state lottery that brought in money to the state coffers, as did increases in the state's gasoline tax. The economy in general and in Connecticut improved, and people within the government were spending state money more judiciously. All of this resulted in the state's generating a budget surplus. Grasso hired back most of the employees who had been laid off. She was winning favor but it was not until her tireless effort during the blizzard of 1978 that she could be called a citizen favorite. That she was, however, as was seen in her being reelected by almost 200,000 votes.[10]

A Life Cut Short

In her second term, the budget surplus continued, enabling Grasso to fund some of the initiatives she was most interested in. Her Urban Action Program directed funds to the needs of impoverished areas, with money aimed at housing, mass transit, day care, and services for the elderly. Then things turned again. An oil crisis hit the state's economy and Grasso was

---

[8]Medal of Freedom, http://www.medaloffreedom.com/EllaGrasso.htm

[9]Ella Giovanno Oliva (Tambussi) Grasso, Governor of Connecticut, 1975–1980, Connecticut State Library. http://www.cslib.org/gov/grassoe.htm

[10]Ella Giovanno Oliva (Tambussi) Grasso, Governor of Connecticut, 1975–1980, Connecticut State Library. http://www.cslib.org/gov/grassoe.htm

forced to raise the sales tax to seven-and-a-half percent, one of the highest in the nation. In March of 1980, Grasso was diagnosed with cancer, and at the end of December 1980, she resigned her office. She died in Hartford Hospital on February 5, 1981.[11]

Giving Back

Later that year, President Ronald Reagan posthumously awarded Grasso the Presidential Medal of Freedom, saying: "Governor Ella Grasso was a determined and spirited public servant who brought to her life the energies of the committed. She worked hard to make State government work, and her service to the people of Connecticut was unstinting."[12]

Ella T. Grasso was a plain woman who wore simple clothing and no make-up. Never losing her "down-home" style, she was more interested in helping people than in making a glamorous impression. She lived by the words she spoke: "It is not enough to profess faith in the democratic process; we must do something about it."[13] In doing so, Ella T. Grasso fulfilled her parents' American Dream.

Honors, Awards, and Recognition
- Ella Grasso Highway (Route 75) in Windsor Locks
- State facilities in Groton and Stratford named for her
- Statue of her in south portico of state capitol building
- National Women's Hall of Fame
- Presidential Medal of Freedom
- The Ella Tambussi Grasso Center for Women in Politics
- Connecticut Women's Hall of Fame
- Ella T. Grasso Literary Award, sponsored by UNICO National

[11]Ella Giovanno Oliva (Tambussi) Grasso, Governor of Connecticut, 1975–1980, Connecticut State Library. http://www.cslib.org/gov/grassoe.htm
[12]Laura Elizabeth, "Ella T. Grasso." *Everything*,
http://everything2.com/index.pl?node_id=1426296
[13]"Women of the Hall." National Women's Hall of Fame.
http://www.greatwomen.org/women.php?action=viewone&id=67

photo: Biographical Directory of the United States Congress
http://bioguide.congress.gov/biodisplay.pl?index=g000387

Lido Anthony "Lee" Iacocca
Businessman

In 1978, The Chrysler Corporation was on the verge of bankruptcy. Focusing on large, gas-guzzling vehicles at a time when Americans were facing a costly fuel crisis, the company was bleeding millions of dollars. In addition, its Chrysler F platform vehicles— Dodge Aspen and Plymouth Volare—had to be recalled for costly repairs. If America's third largest auto maker went out of business, thousands of people would lose their jobs and countless others down the food chain would feel the harsh ripple effect of the collapse.

Chrysler brought in Lee Iacocca, recently fired as President at Ford Motor Company, to right the sinking ship. Iacocca immediately announced plant closings and job layoffs. He negotiated with the unions and won some give-backs. To show that the sacrifice would involve everyone connected with the company, Iacocca cut his own salary to $1.00 per year. He cut production on the large unprofitable vehicles and focused the company's efforts on the subcompact Dodge Omni and Plymouth Horizon. Instant hits, these two models reached sales of 300,000 vehicles each in their first year on the market.

Despite these changes, the company still was drowning in red ink and needed operating capital to survive. In 1979, Iacocca took a bold step and went to the United States Congress to ask for the government to guarantee a loan. The government would not be lending the money but guaranteeing lenders that the money would be paid back. As precedent, Iacocca pointed to the government's assistance given to airlines and railroads when they had been in similar straits. He also pointed out the serious impact the company's closure would have on the nation's workers and the economy. With considerable debate and controversy, Congress approved the request, guaranteeing a loan of $1.5 billion.[1]

Working with this cash infusion, Chrysler released in 1981 the first of

---

[1] http://www.scripophily.net/chryscor.html

the K-Car line, the Dodge Aries and Plymouth Reliant. These small, fuel-efficient, and inexpensive vehicles sold well. Two years later Chrysler put on the market its minivan, for which it became a perennial market leader. With these successes, coupled with other cost-savings moves, Chrysler was able to pay back its loan seven years earlier than expected. Under the guidance of Iacocca, thousands of workers kept their jobs and the company was saved.[2]

Lido Anthony Iacocca was born October 25, 1924, in Allentown, Pennsylvania, to Italian immigrants, Nicola and Antoinette Iacocca. Nicola had come to the United States from San Marco, Italy, when he was 12 years old. With only a fourth-grade education, Nicola opened a hot dog stand, sold real estate, and started a rental car business.[3] Lido ("Lee") had a similar penchant for hard work.

Learning the Value of a Dollar

Like most children raised during the years of the Great Depression, Iacocca quickly became aware of the value of a dollar and the tragedy of waste. At ten years old he would bring his little wagon to the grocery store and cart shoppers' packages home for a tip. At 16, he worked long hours in a fruit market.

Unable to enlist in the service for World War II because of an earlier bout of rheumatic fever, Iacocca enrolled in Lehigh University, where he majored in industrial engineering. After graduation he attended Princeton University on the Wallace Memorial Fellowship, after which he went to work for Ford Motor Company. Unhappy working as an engineer, however, he asked for a transfer into sales and marketing. There he was in his element. Sales and marketing was tailor-made for someone with Iacocca's temperament and ambition—to make $10,000 a year by the time he was 25, and then progress to become a millionaire.

Displaying Marketing and Design Savvy

In 1956, the district Iacocca was managing ranked last in sales. Iacocca decided to take drastic action. He conceived the "56 for 56" program.

---

[2]http://en.wikipedia.org/wiki/Lee_Iacocca
[3]http://en.wikipedia.org/wiki/Lee_Iacocca

Under this program, people could buy a new 1956 Ford for twenty percent down and $56.00 a month for 36 months. The program catapulted Iacocca's district into the number one slot in sales. Ford took the program nationwide and brought Iacocca to Dearborn, Michigan, where he quickly moved up the ranks, becoming President of the Ford Division at the age of 40.

Iacocca spearheaded the development of a number of vehicles that made considerable money for Ford and its shareholders. The Fairlane was one of these. Under Iacocca's direction, the car had to be small but large enough to hold a family of four. It would not weigh more than 2500 pounds or cost more than $2,500. It had to appeal to various markets so the consumer would feel comfortable driving the car to church, the drag strip, or the country club.[4]

He was also involved in the design and development of the popular Ford Mustang, an inexpensive but sporty two-door hard-top or convertible, just right for the muscle-car era. Iacocca also supported the development of the Lincoln Continental Mark III. In the late 1960s, he revived the Mercury brand and introduced the Mercury Cougar and Mercury Marquis.

Iacocca became a visible spokesman for Chrysler, even appearing in some of its television commercials. His frank, direct, lay-it-on-the-line style won over television audiences, responding favorably to his challenge that became the tagline of these ads and Chrysler's battle cry—"If you can find a better car . . . buy it."[5]

As successful as he and the company were, Iacocca, who had been named company president in 1970, had numerous run-ins with Henry Ford II. Often these disagreements were over the designs for new vehicles. In 1978, after a year in which Ford posted $2 billion in profits, Iacocca was fired.[6]

When he moved to Chrysler, some of the designs over which he and Henry Ford argued—such as the K-Car line and the minivan—became the bases for some of Chrysler's major successes. He was also responsible for

[4]http://www.stfrancis.edu/ba/ghkickul/stuwebs/bbios/biograph/leeic.htm

[5]http://www.scripophily.net/chryscor.html

[6]http://en.wikipedia.org/wiki/Lee_Iacocca

photo: http://en.wikipedia.org/wiki/Lee_Iacocca

Chrysler's purchase of AMC in 1987, bringing to Chrysler the Jeep Division. Shortly after Iacocca left the company, Chrysler began marketing its Jeep Grand Cherokee, which also became a best-seller.

Giving Back

In 1982, President Ronald Reagan appointed Iacocca to head the Statue of Liberty-Ellis Island Foundation. Iacocca helped raise $170 million in individual and corporate donations to restore the Statue and the abandoned station where his parents and millions of others first set foot on American soil.

Following the death of his wife from diabetes, Iacocca became active in a number of efforts in supporting research to find a cure for the illness. He formed The Iacocca Foundation, which funds promising research projects. He had all of the proceeds of his autobiography, which sold seven million copies, go to the Foundation. In 2000, he founded Olivio Premium Products, products made with or from olive oil, and has all profits donated to diabetes research. He has been an advocate of "Nourish the Children," an initiative of Nu Skin enterprises. He has led the funding campaign to expand his *alma mater,* Lehigh University, into buildings once owned by Bethlehem Steel.

Quotes from Lee Iacocca

The thing that lies at the foundation of positive change, the way I see it, is service to a fellow human being.

The only rock I know that stays steady, the only institution I know that works, is the family.

Apply yourself. Get all the education you can, but then, by God, do something. Don't just stand there; make it happen.

EDMUND D. PELLEGRINO, MD
Physician, Philosopher

After completing St. Francis Xavier High School in Manhattan, Edmund Pellegrino of Newark, New Jersey, graduated summa cum laude *from St. John's University in Jamaica, New York. He then applied to a number of medical schools but was rejected by all of them. In one response was a note that may have explained all of the rejections. One admissions officer wrote that Edmund might "be happier with his own kind." Italians, his academic advisor said, were no more welcome than Jews in the major medical schools.[1]*

Ironically the determination that is part of his heritage was at work. Edmund's father, a salesman in wholesale foods in New York City, was calling on one of his customers who owned a deli near New York University. The elder Pellegrino asked his customer to introduce him to one of the regular patrons who happened to be the dean of NYU Medical School. After hearing of Edmund's plight, the dean suggested Edmund send his records to the dean. Edmund was accepted and went on to become one of the school's most distinguished graduates.

Dr. Edmund D. Pellegrino's career has taken him to many places where he has served in many positions. He was president of Yale-New Haven Medical Center, chancellor and vice president for Health Science at the University of Tennessee, founding chief executive of the Health Science Center at SUNY Stony Brook, founder of the Department of Medicine at the University of Kentucky, and president of the Catholic University of America. He is the John Carroll Professor Emeritus of Medicine and Medical Ethics at Georgetown University.

---

[1]Karen Geraghty, "Guarding the Art: Edmund D. Pellegrino, MD," *American Medical Association*, www.ama-assn.org/ama/pub/category/print/6572.html.

Council on Bioethics

A physician first and foremost, Dr. Pellegrino has made his mark in the area of bioethics, and in October 2005, President George W. Bush named him Chair of the President's Council on Bioethics. He has authored more than 20 books and more than 500 articles on the subject of medical ethics in the treatment of patients, humanism and the physician, and the philosophical basis of medical treatment. He is the founding editor of the *Journal of Medicine and Philosophy.*

Devoting more than 50 years to his field, Dr. Pellegrino saw medicine as a moral endeavor, founded upon the patient-physician covenant. He felt that "people in the healing professions deal with human beings in a state of vulnerability, and it is incumbent upon them to be intellectually honest, competent, and compassionate—and to put the patient's needs first. . . . Healthcare is now a commodity for many. . . . The world desperately needs people dedicated to something beyond their own self-interest."[2]

A Divided Profession

In his writing and speeches, Dr. Pellegrino broached his subject in different ways. In 1997 he said: "As I look to the future, I think we will undoubtedly be a much more divided profession. . . . There will be those (physicians) who choose to follow the moral imperative—the high ground—and those who become purely businessmen and entrepreneurs."

While physicians have the moral obligation to stay informed and educated in the use of new technologies, he wrote, procedures derived from the destruction of human embryos, distortions and bypassing of normal reproductive processes, or cloning of human beings, as well as other "enhancements," are not morally permissible no matter how useful they might be therapeutically.[3]

---

[2]www.marymount.edu/news/news02/march02/032702.html
[3]E. Pellegrino, "Biotechnology, Human Enhancement, and the Ends of Medicine," *The Center for Bioethics and Human Dignity,* Nov. 30, 2004.
www.cbhd.org/resources/biotech/pellegrino_2004-11-30_print.htm

The Misguided Need to Approach Perfection

He speaks of "bodily enhancements" achieved by the physician's intervention that goes beyond the ends of medicine as they have traditionally been held:

> We start with someone who has no disease or obvious bodily malformation. . . . Yet the person feels dissatisfied with her (his) portion in life. She (he) feels unfulfilled, at a social disadvantage, or completely deficient in some mental or physical bodily trait. She (he) may want to augment a state to what she (he) thinks is a normal level, or she (he) may want something approaching perfection. To make physicians into enhancement therapists is to make therapy a happiness nostrum, not a true healing enterprise.[4]

Yet the pressures on physicians are great. They are moved to help patients in need. They are attracted by the lure of huge financial gain. Team trainers want to "help the team win" and so they provide artificial enhancements. But physicians must resist these pressures, despite the apparent good they might bring. Dr. Pellegrino cites the physicians in the Nazi regime who conducted experiments on humans in the name of seeking cures that would benefit all humanity. "They even convinced themselves," Dr. Pellegrino writes, "that their heinous acts were consistent with their nefarious ideals."[5]

Standing Firm

Based on sound moral principles, Dr. Pellegrino's positions have not been popular in some quarters. Yet he has been applauded across the land for holding his ground, supporting his positions with sound scientific and philosophic evidence. In the process, this son of Italian immigrants is giving back to the countless millions of patients and physicians whose lives have been made better because of his contribution.

---

[4]E. Pellegrino, "Biotechnology, Human Enhancement, and the Ends of Medicine."

[5]E. Pellegrino, "The Nazi Doctors and Nuremberg: Some Moral Lessons Revisited," *Annals of Internal Medicine*, Aug. 15, 1997. www.annals.org/cgi/content/fell/127/4/307

photo: http://www.cbhd.org/aboutcbhd/fellows/pellegrino.htm

Honors and Awards
- Recipient of 45 honorary doctoral degrees
- Edmund D. Pellegrino Road at Ambulatory Surgery Center at Stony Brook University named in his honor
- Master of the American College of Physicians
- Fellow of the American Association for the Advancement of Science
- Recipient of the Benjamin Rush Award from the American Medical Association
- Recipient of the Abraham Flexner Award of the Association of American Medical Colleges
- Recipient, the Laetare Award of the University of Notre Dame
- Recipient of the Beecher Award for Life Achievement in Bioethics from The Hastings Center
- Recipient of the Marymount University Ethics Award

HON. MARIE L. GARIBALDI
State Supreme Court Justice

One of the original 13 colonies, New Jersey is *one of the nation's oldest states. Yet not until 1982* *did a woman serve on its State Supreme Court.* *That woman was Marie L. Garibaldi. Upon her re-* *tirement some 20 years later, New Jersey Governor* *Thomas Kean reflected on his appointing Garibaldi* *a State Supreme Court Justice:*

"When I was elected (Governor), I was extraor- *dinarily apprehensive about appointing judges. . . .* *(Yet) I thought it a disgrace that in the long history* *of our state there had never been a woman on our Supreme Court. I wanted* *to appoint the ablest woman in the legal profession in the state of New Jersey.* *. . .*

"It was important to me that the first female New Jersey Supreme Court *Justice would be well qualified. I did not want anyone to allege that she was* *there only because she was a woman. . . . Everyone thought Marie was a su-* *perb appointment, and she was superb on the court."[1]*

Strong Family Influences

Marie L. Garibaldi was born in Jersey City, New Jersey, in a family that provided the foundation for her future achievements. Her father was a physician who urged the hospital at which he worked, St. Francis Hospital, to hire its first woman doctor. Marie was about 12 years old at the time and this event made a strong impression on her. Marie's mother influenced her, too, as she had been the bookkeeper for the family business since she was only 14 years old.

---

[1]Thomas Kean, "Justice Marie Garibaldi: Simply the Best," *Seton Hall Law Review* 31:1.

Marie attended private school through 12ᵗʰ grade. When she graduated from Connecticut College, she wanted to pursue a career in business, but the most prestigious business schools were not accepting women. So Marie applied to law school, thinking this would be an alternate route into business. She was one of 12 females in a class of 253 students at Columbia Law School. Even with her law degree, however, Marie found Wall Street closed to her. Thus began her career in law.

Working Her Way Up

She spent six years with the IRS, prosecuting civil tax fraud cases in Tax Court. She left government service in part because of the Hatch Political Activities Act, which restricted government employees from making political speeches or writing articles on political issues.

Ms. Garibaldi worked for two different law firms, becoming a partner at Riker, Danzig, Scherer, Hyland & Perretti after just three years. In addition to her work there, she served as a municipal court judge in Weehawken, New Jersey. There she earned a reputation for being "unaffected in her demeanor," for managing "to keep calm even with heavily emotional cases," and for always being "incredibly fair" in hearing the evidence and rendering her opinions.

Joining the New Jersey State Bar Association, she quickly assumed leadership roles. First she chaired its Section on Taxation. Later she was Association Secretary and then moved on to become the President—the first woman to hold that position.

Justice Garibaldi

In 1982, Marie L. Garibaldi took the oath of office as an Associate Justice of the New Jersey Supreme Court. During her 17 years on the Court, Justice Garibaldi wrote more than 225 opinions covering widely disparate areas of the law. Her opinions have been regarded as being thoughtful and concise, and particularly useful in guiding lower courts.

----

[2]"Justice Marie L. Garibaldi Announces Her Retirement from the Supreme Court," http://www.judiciary.state.nj.us/pressrel/p991222.htm

"A number of themes emerged from Justice Garibaldi's decisions and opinions. When evaluating cases before the high court, for example, she tempered her critical legal analysis with a healthy dose of good common sense."[3] In this regard, former New Jersey Supreme Court Justice Robert L. Clifford said:

> Frequently, when the court's conferences focused on differing views on some esoteric principle of law, Justice Garibaldi would bring us back to earth. She always wanted to know how our decisions would play out in the real world. She would ask how it was going to work on the street.[4]

At the same time, Justice Garibaldi supported her decisions with information drawn from sociological studies, government investigations, and law review articles that evaluated emerging social trends.

To Resolve, Not to Legislate

Justice Garibaldi felt strongly that the Court's role is to resolve disputes, not legislate. Her opinions demonstrate her dedication to upholding the separation of powers among the three branches of government.

Justice Garibaldi carefully limited the court's role when handling sensitive personal issues. In three right-to-die cases, her opinions recognized that respect for human life must be balanced against human dignity and individual choice. Her compassion is obvious, reflecting an understanding of the "anguish that family members experience in determining when to disconnect life support systems." For one case she wrote: "We emphasize that in this case as in every case, the ultimate decision is not for the Court. The decision is primarily that of the patient, competent or incompetent, and the patient's family or guardian and physician."[5]

Another of her decisions that carried widespread application dealt with sexual harassment in the work environment. In her opinion, Justice Garibaldi announced a new three-part "test in the hope of creating a stan-

---

[3]Linda Pissott Reig, "A Tribute to the Honorable Marie L. Garibaldi," *Seton Hall Law Review* 31:4.

[4]Harvey Fisher and Scott Goldstein, "Garibaldi Retiring; LaVecchia Named," *New Jersey Law* 2712 (Dec. 27, 1999).

[5]Pissott Reig.

dard that both employees and employers will be able to understand and one that employers can realistically enforce." The opinion provided ample guidance so future litigants could understand what proofs are required to prevail on a sexual harassment claim.[6]

Balance and Recognition

Her sense of awareness and need for balance are evident in her opinions. Among these are opinions that:

- Recognize that police officers place their lives in jeopardy to promote public safety. One decision in particular supported police in search and seizure and privacy matters.
- Protect free speech, even when it is "extremely repulsive and hateful." Justice Garibaldi stated: "[a]s a society we have made a determination that the best way to combat bias and prejudice is through the exchange of ideas and speech, not through lawsuits." The Justice recognized that free speech does have boundaries and saw the need to balance freedom of speech against the protection of a person's reputation.[7]

Mentor, Teacher, and Friend

In her years on the bench, Justice Garibaldi never lost her connection to people. It would not be unusual, for example, for her to sit in her office sharing lunch with her secretary and clerks. Serving as mentor to numerous clerks, she engaged in hearty debate with them over various legal issues before the court. As her parents had done for her, Justice Garibaldi helped prepare many clerks and others—men and women—to build successful careers, within and outside the legal profession.

A former clerk wrote these words about her mentor:

I distinctly remember when my high school teacher announced in history class: "Today the first woman, Marie L. Garibaldi, was appointed to the

---

[6]Pissott Reig.
[7]Pissott Reig.

New Jersey Supreme Court." I remember thinking that it could not possibly be true. In all the years that our court system existed, it was hard
to believe that no other woman had been appointed to this State's highest
court. . . . I have firsthand knowledge that Justice Garibaldi is easily one
of the finest jurists, male or female, in New Jersey's history.[8]

---

[8]Pissott Reig.

photo: http://www.niaf.org/about/board_officers.asp?print=i&

Anthony J. Fornelli
Lawyer, Publisher

*Anthony J. Fornelli has served at every level of gov-
ernment in his home state of Illinois; presided over half
a dozen non-profits; raised or donated well over a million dollars for charity; and earned nearly a dozen
local, national and international honors. But some of
his fondest memories—and most valuable life lessons—date back to a small park in Chicago.*

*"I grew up in the Our Lady of Angels Parish on the
'Great West Side' and as kids we all hung out at Ryerson
Playground. In the summer, we'd play baseball, basketball and checkers, and
in the winter they flooded the field and we played ice hockey, or we'd shovel
away the snow and play football from morning until night.*

*"We were a mix of Italian, Slav, Irish, German, and Jewish and—miracle
of miracles—we all got along. We'd kid around about our backgrounds, of
course, but there were no gang wars or fights because of ethnicity. We respected each other's differences and that really stuck with me."*

Learning the Importance of Work and Education

Anthony J. "Tony" Fornelli was born two days after Italo Balbo's tri-
umphant arrival in Chicago. The Italian Air Force general had led a
squadron of 24 Savoia Marchetti seaplanes across the Atlantic in the summer of 1933, landing on Lake Michigan to international acclaim on July 15
during Chicago's Century of Progress World's Fair. "My father went down
to see him, like every other good Italian at the time," Fornelli recalls. "The
next day, my mother went into labor and I was born just after midnight. I
was nicknamed 'Balbo' for a couple of years. The joke was that the stork
brought everyone else, but Balbo brought me."

Tony was the only child of Gennaro Fornelli, who hailed from Naples,
and Madelyn (Cimino), who "hailed from Calabria by way of Des Moines,
Iowa." An insurance salesman for most of his career, Gennaro worked
three jobs during the Depression: as a drug store clerk, in a picture-frame

factory, and as a door-to-door brush salesman. Except for a stint at Standard Coil Co. during World War II, Madelyn was a homemaker who had unshakable aspirations for her son.

"In those days, there weren't that many people pursuing a higher education, but since I was 6 years old, I can remember my mother saying, 'You're going to college.' When I got older, my dad would say, 'He doesn't have to go to college if he doesn't want to,' and my mother would come back with, 'Oh, yes he does,' and that was that."

An academic standout at Our Lady of Angels Grade School and a scholar/athlete at St. Ignatius Preparatory School, Fornelli credits instructors at each school with keeping him on the straight and narrow. At Our Lady of the Angels, it was his seventh grade teacher, Sr. Mary Ellenette, BVM. "She singled me out as a student with some promise and she would have long talks with me after class. I told her once that I wanted to work in a drug store and she said, 'Oh no, no, no. You're going to a good high school and then you're going on to a good college.' She and my mother were in cahoots in that regard."

At St. Ignatius, it was the school's football and track coach, Ralph Mailliard. "Mal was the kind of guy who knew how to pat a guy on the back or kick him in the ass, and when to do which. He'd pat me on the back and I'd run through a brick wall for him."

A star sprinter on a track team that won the city championships eight years in a row, Mailliard was also a varsity halfback who would roll right over a tackler if he couldn't run around him. But it was off the field that Mailliard had the greatest influence. A history and philosophy instructor at St. Ignatius, he was legendary for driving down Roosevelt Road with a carload of students in tow, regaling them with stories or engaging them in conversations about life's great mysteries.

"I remember we were all having a hard time getting our arms around the concept of faith and free will, so there we were, driving down Roosevelt Road, with Mal explaining what free will was all about. You knew you were somebody when you got to be a passenger in Mal's car."

Fornelli graduated from St. Ignatius with honors and headed off to Marquette University on a football scholarship. But a season-ending injury left him sidelined and discouraged, and he returned home after his freshman year.

Undaunted, he went into business for himself; married his high school sweetheart, Angela Favia; and began raising a family that would grow to include five daughters. When his spray painting and metal manufacturing businesses went under, he took a job driving a meat truck, while he pursued an undergraduate degree at Loyola University and a law degree at DePaul University.

"I got the job (at the meat packing plant) through my brother-in-law, Phil, and I was given a great deal of latitude by my boss, David Fagel, to get back in time to attend class. I would get up at 4:30 in the morning and go to work, drive the truck until 3:30 p.m., attend class in the evening, stay up until midnight studying, sleep for four hours, then get up and do it all over again."

Facing Adversity

In 1958, tragedy befell his beloved neighborhood. "I was out making deliveries in my truck when I got a call from my father-in-law, who told me to come on back. When I got in, they told me that there was 'a problem' at the school and they couldn't find my daughter, Madelyn."

The "problem" was a horrific fire that ravaged Our Lady of Angels Grade School. Luckily, Fornelli's daughter was attending kindergarten in an auxiliary building that was untouched by the fire. School officials released all the children from their classes when the calamity struck and "Madelyn was blissfully walking down Chicago Avenue when my sister-in-law and wife found her."

Other families weren't so lucky. The fire took the lives of 92 students and three teachers and tore the heart out of the close-knit community. "The fire destroyed our pastor, Monsignor Cussen—he never was the same after that—and ultimately it destroyed the neighborhood."

A Lawyer on the Rise

Fornelli completed his education and launched his legal career. In the process, he developed a reputation for hard work and integrity that he maintained throughout his life and that has kept him in good stead every step of the way.

"I was clerking for an attorney named Roger Maritote right out of law school when I was approached by Chuck Winkler, with whom I had studied for the bar in 1960. He told me, 'My father (who was a Chicago police officer) says that I have to go into practice with you because your heart's in the right place.' That was the start of a 17-year partnership."

From that point on, Fornelli's career has been a complex tapestry of professional, political, civic, and charitable involvement, with each thread complementing the other.

As an assistant attorney for Chicago's corporation counsel, Fornelli defended the rights of the city's police officers.

As a leader of the Chicago Amerital Chapter of UNICO National, an Italian-American service organization with scores of chapters in a dozen states, Fornelli chaired Festa Italiana along Chicago's lakefront for 18 years. The annual celebration raised more than $1 million for a variety of charities, including the Neediest Children's Fund, Italian Earthquake Relief, the American Jewish Committee, and Cooley's anemia research.

As a rising star in the Joint Civic Committee of Italian Americans, an umbrella organization of several dozen Chicago-area groups, Fornelli attained the post of president in 1974, serving along the way as chairman of the organization's Human Relations Committee.

When Frank Annunzio, then a fledgling congressman from the 7th District, was gerrymandered out of the 7th District in 1972, Fornelli helped run the campaign that would win the 11th District for Annunzio, a position he held for more than two decades.

Fornelli was rewarded for his loyalty in 1973 when Illinois Governor Dan Walker appointed him director of the Department of Financial Institutions, a cabinet-level position charged with overseeing credit unions, currency exchanges and unclaimed property.

In 1976, he began a nine-year stint as a member of the Chicago Plan Commission, the adjudicating body charged with determining the best uses of property in Chicago. And in 1988, he began a seven-year tenure with the city's Zoning Board of Appeals, which reviews requests for zoning variances.

Though Fornelli served as director of the Department of Financial Institutions for only two years, he earned the lasting respect of the industry. In 1977, he was invited to become a partner in a small chain of currency exchanges that he helped grow to 50 outlets in three states in less than a decade. Today, Fornelli is a director of the Illinois Community Currency

Exchange Association and either owns or has an interest in nearly a dozen currency exchanges and 50 payday loan outlets.

Serving the Italian-American Community

Fornelli's impact on the Chicago-area Italian-American community has been immeasurable.

After the 1990 Census, when the only two US congressmen to be redistricted out of office were Italian Americans, Fornelli and several other community leaders "heard the call." They formed the Italian American Political Coalition to restore the community to its rightful place in the state's political landscape.

In 1996, when the community was in danger of losing its main communication vehicle, *Fra Noi,* Fornelli organized a group of investors that returned the paper to solvency. He currently serves as publisher of the thriving monthly newspaper.

In 1999, Fornelli and a handful of other community leaders negotiated a lease with the Missionaries of St. Charles to convert the Sacred Heart Seminary into Casa Italia, a community center for Chicago-area Italian Americans.

In 2005, Fornelli founded the Italian American Veterans Museum and Library at Casa Italia. Dedicated to honoring Italian-American bravery from the Revolutionary War to the present, the IAVML produced a documentary in 2008 exploring the impact of World War II on the Chicago-area Italian American community.

In addition to the Joint Civic Committee of Italian Americans, Fornelli has presided over UNICO National, Chicago Amerital Chapter of UNICO, Justinian Society of Lawyers, Italian American Political Coalition, and Casa Italia. He has been honored by the JCCIA, Justinians, Gregorians (a society of Italian educators), Italian American Executives of Transportation, and Italian Cultural Center.

Serving the Community at Large

In the larger community, Fornelli has served on the boards of the Jane Addams Hull-House Museum, International Museum of Surgical Science and Hall of Fame, National Hemophilia Foundation, and Austin School for the Mentally Disabled. He has been honored by the Illinois State Bar Association, City of Hope, National Institute of Human Relations, the National Hemophilia Foundation, and the Prime Minister of Israel.

A member of the St. Ignatius Hall of Fame, Fornelli donates generously to a needs-based scholarship bearing his name that's given annually to a student athlete. "I was at a golf outing recently and a fellow came up to me and said, 'You don't know me but I went to St. Ignatius because of you. I saw you at the football games and the way you played made me want to go there.' That made me feel great," Fornelli said.

When he was named a laureate of the Academy of Illinois Lawyers, his longtime friend and protégé, Leonard Amari, said of him: "There are few other men or women who have done more for the legal profession or the Italian American community than Tony Fornelli. He has served as a role model, mentor and friend, and certainly one of the true leaders for well over four decades."

Reaching Out

Fornelli's ability to move seamlessly from the Italian-American community to the larger community came to the attention of David Roth, the Midwest Director of the American Jewish Committee, who invited Fornelli to join the fledgling Illinois Ethnic Coalition in 1976. The idea was to create a team of ethnic diplomats who represented the need of their community and went back into their communities to rally support for the causes of others.

Over the next three decades, Fornelli took part in a steady stream of press conferences and seminars that spotlighted the concerns of every conceivable ethnic group. When 70 White, Black, Hispanic, and Asian leaders met in 1983 to commemorate the 50th anniversary of Stalin's manmade famine in Ukraine, Fornelli addressed the assemblage: "In getting together like this, we realize that our problems aren't unique to our community, that they transcend ethnic barriers. All of us have found similarities in history, outlook and goals."

Though the coalition disbanded in 2005, Anthony J. Fornelli still holds dear its principles—and the lessons he learned at a small park on the West Side of Chicago:

I really believe that if you remain insular as an ethnic community you aren't going to go anywhere. You have to reach out to other people and make their causes yours and vice versa. What binds us together is far greater than what separates us, so if you hurt a Jewish American, for example, or an Asian or Hispanic, you're really hurting every ethnic group.

---

*Contributor to this profile: Paul Basile, *Fra Noi*

Photo: *Fra Noi*

MARYLOU TIBALDO-BONGIORNO
JEROME BONGIORNO
Filmmakers

In the film, Little Kings, *three Santello broth-ers—Italian Americans—are talking.*

DOM: How can you expect to have a good relationship with your wife when you're doing someone on the side?

GINO: We're Italian.

Photo: © Bongiorno Productions, Inc.

DOM: Okay, hold it right there. What is this? You always say that. 'We're Italian.' What the hell does that mean?

GINO: Don Corleone, Al Capone, Caligula, Casanova....

DOM: Degenerates. All degenerates.

GINO: Stupid, these people lived large. Life is too short.

DOM (to JOHNNY): You agree with him?

JOHNNY: He's not wrong.

DOM: Johnny, I'm disappointed in you.

JOHNNY: Dom, calm down.

DOM: I'm not going to calm down. That's not what being Italian should mean to you. We're not gangsters. We're not immoral. Now if you say ... Dante, Michelangelo, DaVinci ... then ...

Jerome Bongiorno sees himself as part of the classic Italian-American experience. In 1950, his father, Peter Bongiorno, emigrated with little education from Sicily at age 17. He settled in Brooklyn, joined the bricklayers' union, married a Brooklyn-born, Italian-American woman, Patricia Coppola, and saw to it that his three children were educated at Catholic schools. Jerome then experienced the next part of the Italian-American

---

[1]From *Little Kings,* by Marylou Tibaldo-Bongiorno and Jerome Bongiorno, Emmy-nominated. Award-winning husband and wife filmmakers.

journey—the family moved from Brooklyn to suburban Staten Island. He was educated by Christian Brothers in high school and then by Jesuits in college, where he met his future wife, Marylou Tibaldo.

After majoring in biology in college, Jerome spent two years in medical school. He then decided to teach high school science by day and play/record original music with his rock band by night, in addition to pursuing painting and drawing. Then he made a right turn into filmmaking—not a typical career for the son of a working-class, Italian-American family. Jerome says: "To my family, filmmaking was like going to Mars."

Marylou Tibaldo–Bongiorno's father, Angelo L. Tibaldo, emigrated from Montecchio in Northern Italy with his family. The year was 1936 and he was six years old. The family lived first in Newark, New Jersey, and then moved to nearby Belleville. Angelo worked in a local leather factory. While stationed overseas in the Air Force, he met and married an Italian woman, Paolina Peloso, from his parents' home town of Montorso. The couple settled in Newark, in a neighborhood filled with relatives. He educated both of his children at Catholic schools. Marylou earned scholarships to Queen of Peace High School and Saint Peter's College.

In college, Marylou, too, majored in biology and that's where she met Jerome. After graduation, she spent two years in a neurophysiology doctoral program, but decided to teach high school science in a prep school and write and produce plays with Jerome. In 1986, they were married at the Cathedral Basilica of the Sacred Heart in the city where they settled—Newark, NJ.

While they were writing and directing one of their plays, an actor suggested they make a film together. They did, and the couple was "hooked." In 1994, Marylou enrolled full time in NYU's Graduate Film School. In 1999, the Bongiornos formed their own production company, Bongiorno Productions, and produced award winning, cutting edge fictional and documentary films. They refer to themselves as a "two-person band"—Marylou raises the money and directs; Jerome shoots and edits. They write their screenplays together. They often use their documentary films as research for their fictional stories. Marylou explains that approach with a quote from director Jean-Luc Godard: "In filmmaking, you can either start with fiction or documentary, but whichever you start with, you inevitably find the other."

Of Sons and Mothers

While their filmmaking technique developed from their varied experiences—theater, music, painting, drawing—the content and themes of their films reflect their Italian-American experience: first-generation, Catholic, and family-oriented. It all served not only as a sense memory to inform what they created but also to inspire them thematically.

For example, Marylou and Jerome made *Mother Tongue,* a short documentary that featured Jerome's cousins, who are mother/son restaurateurs. Documentary filmmakers are told to "shoot what you know," Marylou said, so she and Jerome "looked in our backyard and to the riches of our Italian-American family." That film led to an expanded 43-minute version that further explored the complex Italian-American mother/son bond. It featured comments from seven men and their mothers, including director Martin Scorsese, Mayor Rudy Giuliani, actor John Turturro, and singer Pat DiNizio of the "Smithereens." *Mother Tongue: Italian American Sons and Mothers* earned an Emmy nomination and revealed that the Italian-American mother/son relationship is very passionate. The mothers in this film are very opinionated about their sons' lives, particularly their ultimate career paths. Many times they disagreed with their sons' choices but they stayed right beside them each step of the way.

For instance, DiNizio tells of his band's endless round of playing "noisy and horrendous" nightclubs, with a familiar face in the audience—his mother. Fans christened her "Mother of the Smithereens," of which she is proud. In the film she speaks lovingly of the spaghetti and meatball dinners she fed to the band when they rehearsed in her basement at top volume for seven years. She also talks on film of the sacrifices her son had to make because he chose to be a musician rather than hold a secure job in the family sanitation business.

"Of course, I see my own Italian-American mother, Jerome's mother, all my aunts and grandmothers in the mothers of these men," Marylou said. Jerome added: "Marylou has always been fascinated by the dynamics between my mother and me. When we don't get along, it's explosive. When we do get along, it's magic. Those times contain all the ambition, emotion, and passion that Italians had when they uprooted themselves from their country and came to America."

We're Italian

Another of the couple's films with an Italian-American theme is *Little Kings*. It tells a simple story of three Italian-American brothers with complicated love lives, their interactions, failings, triumphs, and discoveries. In a very revealing scene, the brothers are arguing about one's (Gino's) dissolute behavior, particularly his marital infidelity. Gino defends himself by saying "We're Italian," pointing to role models with the names Don Corleone, Al Capone, Caligula, and Casanova. "All degenerates," his younger brother, Dom, says. He adds: "That's not what being Italian should mean to you. We're not gangsters; we're not immoral."

In *Little Kings*, the Bongiornos pay homage to Fellini's *Amarcord*, Bertolucci's *The Conformist*, Visconti's *Rocco and His Brothers*, and "some Quentin Tarantino and Woody Allen for innovation and humor."

In their films, Marylou and Jerome portray what they see as the best qualities of Italian Americans—"Not being afraid to show our emotions, being sensual, and exhibiting passion."

Film critic Sherry Mazzochi wrote of *Little Kings*: "There are the requisite scenes of family dinners overflowing with pasta, wine, and yelling relatives. But she (Tibaldo-Bongiorno) has crafted a movie that is as fresh and appealing as its youthful cast." The cast member who plays Gino, Mark Giordano, added some insight to an understanding of the film's theme when he said that when he auditions for parts, he is often told he's "not blue-collar enough and too intelligent" to play an Italian American."[2] Jerome Bongiorno responds: "Nobody plays an Italian American like an Italian American. Too often it's really disappointing to watch a film about Italian American characters where the actors, if they're not Italian American themselves, or if they're being directed by someone who's not Italian American, wind up acting coarse, with a *cafone* attitude."

Revolution '67

Besides mining the Italian-American experience, the Bongiornos also focus on challenges of social change. Once again, they did not have to go far to find a subject. One of Marylou's lifelong passions, which Jerome now shares, is her love for Newark, New Jersey. She grew up there and has lived there with Jerome since they were married. Many of her contemporaries have abandoned this city of poverty, crime, and widespread neglect.

As a means of giving back, the Bongiornos work to find solutions to the city's problems. But first they needed to understand how the city came to be one of the nation's most troubled. Marylou and Jerome decided to turn back to the summer of 1967. It was a time when riots raged in Los Angeles, Detroit, and other cities, as well as Newark. The Newark Riots smoldered for six days and took the lives of 26 people. Some 725 were injured, and approximately 1,500 people were arrested.

Their 90-minute film—*Revolution '67*—incorporates powerful archival news footage, animation, and interviews with activists, the former state governor and city mayor, journalists, a former National Guard member, historians, and eyewitnesses, with a jazz soundtrack.[3] All cities have high population densities," the film says, "but when poverty is prevalent, the city deteriorates: crime, low graduation rates, corrupt government—Newark." The Bongiornos have come to understand that the only solution for Newark is to reduce the poverty. That can be done in one of two ways: gentrify the city and move the poor out, or, their goal, rehabilitate the city by creating jobs and a middle class. "This requires empowerment," they said, "and constant pressure on the political structure. You can't take 'no jobs' for an answer."

Revolution '67 was broadcast nationally on the premier PBS non-fiction series P.O.V., where it was seen by more than a million viewers. It has won international prizes, two national awards for outstanding film of American history, and is on a college and community tour, being shown to diverse audiences around the world.

You Can't Take "No" for an Answer
In a very challenging industry, Marylou and Jerome Bongiorno know they have their work cut out for them. But like their ancestors before them, they will not shy away from the challenge:

---

[3]http://blog.nj.com/ledgernewark/2007/06/revolutionary_viewpoint.html

Notes from Marylou Tibaldo-Bongiorno

Making films aimed at social change is especially challenging. To produce these films, we rely on the enlightened, progressive leadership of foundations, corporations, and government sponsorship. Many times, in order to secure grants we have to suffer initial rejections. We must go back many times. You can't take 'no' for an answer.

A New Breed of Filmmakers

At a time when movies and television seem determined to portray Italian Americans as negative stereotypes, the work of Marylou Tibaldo-Bongiorno and Jerome Bongiorno offers a refreshing and truthful alternative. Upcoming projects include *Watermark,* a love story set in Venice, Italy, and post-Katrina New Orleans, the fictional version of *Revolution '67,* which is being executive-produced by Spike Lee, and a documentary about eco-sustainable housing.

AMADEO OBICI
Businessman

Only 12 years old and not knowing a word of Eng-
lish, Amadeo Obici left his home in Oderzo, Italy, and
headed for America. Instructions on his destination
were pinned to his coat. His uncle was supposed to meet
the boy in Scranton, Pennsylvania, but Amedeo got off
the train at Wilkes-Barre, PA. Frightened and confused,
the little boy began to cry. A policeman, so the legend
goes, tried to calm the boy down by giving him a hand-
ful of peanuts. How ironic! This young boy grew up to
found and operate one of the largest peanut businesses in the world.[1]

Off to America

When Amadeo was just seven years old, his father, Pietro, a saddle-maker in Oderzo, Italy, died, leaving a widow, Luigia, and four children. Luigia had to sell the family business, and Amadeo, the eldest child, took work as a tinsmith's apprentice. At age 11, however, his uncle in America (Luigia's brother) suggested that the boy could do better in the United States. So off he went, with the plan to make enough money to have, at some point, his mother and siblings join him. He went to school in Scranton and worked at a cigar factory before seeking greater opportunities in Wilkes-Barre.[2]

Having a Knack for Business

There he worked at a number of jobs, including a fruit stand. Very perceptive, with a knack for business, Obici saw many buyers of fruit also choosing peanuts for a snack. He stored that fact away in his mind for the right time. Meanwhile he continued working and saving. He built his own

[1]http://goodthingsitalian.blogspot.com/2007/10/jeopardy-answer-amadeo-obici-and-mario_

[2]http://www.newsday.com/news/dp-21415sy0ssep11,0,284664.story

roaster from spare parts and operated a pushcart business selling peanuts. Obici had a natural flair for promotion. Every bag of roasted peanuts that he sold contained a letter of his last name—O-B-I-C-I. The letter O appeared in one out of every 50 bags. Customers who found a letter O would win a free watch. Over time, he gave away more than 20,000 watches.[3] His promotions must have been effective, however, because seven years after his arrival, he had saved up enough money for passage for his mother and two siblings. The family was together again.

Obici developed a new way to blanch the nuts, "taking away the hulls and skins." He dubbed himself "The Peanut Specialist."[4] In 1906, he convinced Mario Peruzzi—a friend and his future brother-in-law—to join him in forming Planters Peanut Company in Scranton. Two years later the company was incorporated as Planters Nut and Chocolate Company.

Seeing Obici's success, his landlords raised his rent. Obici responded by buying his own buildings. When he saw the cost of paper increasing steadily, he bought tracks of timber and processed his own paper. He produced his own tin for the early Planters Peanuts cans.[5] Always eager to cut out the middleman when doing so was feasible, Obici moved the manufacturing side of the company to Suffolk, Virginia, where most of the peanuts were bought.

Mr. Peanut Is Born

Good companies have logos to enhance brand recognition, and Obici wanted a logo, or icon, for his company. Rather than commission a professional artist, he created a marketing gimmick. He sponsored a drawing contest. Participants submitted original sketches they thought reflected the company. One of those sketches was the basis for the world-renowned Mr. Peanut. The character was the creation of a 13-year-old boy named Anthony Gentile. A company artist refined it, adding the monocle, cane, and top hat. Others modified it over the years to adapt to the times.[6]

---

[3] http://goodthingsitalian.blogspot.com_
[4] http://www.obicihcf.org/founder.html
[5] http://goodthingsitalian.blogspot.com_
[6] http://www.obicihcf.org/founder.html

More than a Five-Dollar Prize

The prize the teenager won for creating Mr. Peanut was a mere five dollars. But later Obici helped put the boy through college and medical school. He also financed the college educations of many other area students, and he secretly covered hospital bills for friends and employees. He had a hospital built in Oderzo named after his mother.

Sharing with His Extended Family

Obici married Louise Musante in Scranton, and the couple moved to Suffolk. There they eventually lived in an 1870s farmhouse that they remodeled and expanded. Besides providing jobs for local residents at Planters, the couple was very generous toward the people of the town. Though they could not have children of their own, they often held events at their estate for local children. Civic and military groups were invited for visits to their home, and a clubhouse was built on their estate to be used by Planters' employees for their recreation.

After Louise died in 1938, Obici created a trust fund for the construction of a 138-bed hospital in her name—the Louise Obici Memorial Hospital. Money from the trust fund benefited the hospital and the Suffolk community for the next 50 years. A statement put out by what is now the Obici Healthcare Foundation said: "Amadeo Obici was one of the area's most important philanthropists, a man who came to his new homeland with nothing, built a successful business, and generously shared his success with his Suffolk neighbors."[7]

---

[7]http://www.obicihcf.org/founder.html

photo: Obici Healthcare Foundation

ROCCO A. PETRONE
NASA Director

Rocco Petrone was a demanding NASA executive who played a major role in the Apollo manned spaceflights to the moon. His insistence on the highest quality is exemplified in this comment by Humboldt C. Mandell, Jr., a retired NASA manager at Johnson Space Center in Houston:

NASA was grilling the contractor people on some program delays. Rocco was the one who was never content with an answer, and kept probing one young contractor engineer, who quickly reached the limit of his knowledge. Instead of admitting it, he tried to bluff. Bad mistake. Rocco took him physically off the podium, and told the young man's boss to take the podium. He also told the boss that the young man was to be removed from the program. Brutal? Maybe, but it made us all know our subjects thoroughly from then on.[1]

Rocco Anthony Petrone was born in upstate New York, in a town called Amsterdam. Both of his parents emigrated from Sasso di Castalta in Basilicata. His father was a railroad laborer; his mother worked in a glove factory. When Rocco was a baby, his father died in a work-related accident. A few years later, Rocco would be found delivering ice to help support his family.

Cadet Petrone
Upon completing high school, he won an appointment to the US Military Academy at West Point. There he excelled, even playing tackle on the

[1] http://www.washingtonpost.com/wp-dyn/content/article/2006/08/30/AR2006083003221
_p. . . . .

football team that included two Heisman Trophy winners—Doc Blanchard and Glenn Davis.

After serving three years in Germany, he earned a master's degree in mechanical engineering from Massachusetts Institute of Technology. He then worked on various missile programs, including the nation's first, the Redstone ballistic missile.[2] This was the vehicle used to propel America's first astronauts, Alan Shepard and Virgil "Gus" Grissom, on their suborbital missions.[3]

On to NASA

Petrone then went to NASA in 1960 on loan from the Army. Working from what became the Kennedy Space Center in Florida, he took over planning, development, and activation of all launch facilities for the Saturn launch rockets, which were instrumental to the Apollo lunar missions.[4] He was described in a *Washington Post* article as "a broad-shouldered tree of a man who in his line of work is treated with the same mixture of awe and respect football players give Vince Lombardi (legendary coach)."[5]

In 1967, "he was present during the capsule fire aboard what is often called Apollo 1, and the death of the three astronauts had a lasting effect on Petrone's unremitting manner when it came to quality control," said Roger D. Launius, chairman of the space history division of the National Air and Space museum.[6] Petrone later said of this tragedy:

When the cry came out, I looked at the screen. I saw something going on. I saw a shake, I saw a flash inside the ship. It was just utter helplessness. Just nothing you could do. You could not get to them. The thing exploded in 19 seconds.... Those minutes were heart-rending.[7]

Man on the Moon

Petrone played a major role in 1969 when Apollo 11 landed on the

---

[2]http://www.space.com/news/ap_rocco_petrone.html

[3]http://www.nasa.gov/vision/space/features/rocco_petrone.html

[4]http://www.space.com/news/ap_rocco_petrone.html

[5]http://www.nasa.gov/vision/space/features/rocco_petrone.html

[6]http://www.washingtonpost.com/wp-dyn/content/article/2006/08/30/AR2006083003221_p. . . .

[7]http://www.space.com/news/ap_rocco_petrone.html

moon and Neil Armstrong took his historic leap for mankind. That year, Petrone was named Director of the entire Apollo program.

In 1973, he became Director of the Marshall Center in Alabama, overseeing the Center's role in Skylab, the nation's first crewed space station. A year later he accepted an appointment as a NASA associate administrator at the agency's headquarters in Washington. He retired in 1975, but in 1981 he went to work for Rockwell International, a California-based defense contractor that built space shuttles. As chief of the space transportation and systems division, he oversaw shuttle design, testing, and manufacture.

The Challenger Tragedy

On the morning of January 28, 1986, the shuttle Challenger was scheduled to launch. Petrone tried to have the launch delayed. His chief objection was that subfreezing weather the night before could have damaged the Challenger's thermal protection tiles. Space agency officials overrode Petrone's objection. Shortly after takeoff, the Challenger exploded and seven astronauts died. Subsequent findings showed that the disaster resulted not from ice, but from the failure of the safety seals known as O-rings within the solid rocket boosters, the two gigantic thrusters that lift the shuttle. It is thought that the failure of the O-rings was cold-induced.[8]

Petrone's Way

Working with and in government agencies often requires persuasive skill to get the funding needed for projects. Petrone was "particularly gifted" in explaining the space agency's needs to visiting dignitaries and political figures. According to Kurt Debus, Kennedy Space Center Director, Petrone asked for fresh batteries for Apollo 11 during launch testing. Few of his colleagues felt this expense would be approved. The reply that came back from Washington was: "If Petrone wants it that way, then do it that way."[9]

---

[8]http://www.washingtonpost.com/wp-dyn/content/article/2006/08/30/AR2006083003221
_p...
[9]http://www.washingtonpost.com/wp-dyn/content/article/2006/08/30/AR2006083003221
_p...

Photo: NASA. http://www.astronautix.com/astros/petrone.htm

ROSA PONSELLE
Operatic Diva

After Rosa finished singing popular music in a café one evening, "an elderly Neapolitan woman gave . . . me . . . a well-worn copy of the score to Mascagni's Cavelleria Rusticana *with the pages of the character Santuzza's dramatic moment,* 'Voi lo sapete, o Momma!' *carefully encircled. It was the first opera score I had ever seen, and the very first aria I was to learn. When I sang it, I felt the full size of my voice open up, in ways so different from what I had experienced in popular-music performing. I had always suspected that my voice was bigger than average, but Miss Ryan, afraid that I might damage my voice if I sang very loudly, never allowed me to approach full volume. Mascagni's powerful* Cavelleria *made me aware of the true size of my singing, and . . . I soon found I had no trouble dwarfing the 20-piece orchestra that accompanied me." (Rosa Ponselle)*[1]

Rosa Ponselle's father, Benardino Ponzillo, was an Italian "from the boot." He was born in Caserta, though his roots lay in Naples. He was attracted to the beautiful Maddelena Conti, also from Caserta. She was 12 years younger than he, and her family's social standing was much higher than his. In fact, an arrangement had been made for her to marry a cooper's son, closer to Maddelena in age as well as status. But Benardino wooed her and won her. In 1885, they left for America, though not yet married, along with Maddelena's parents. They settled near relatives in Sch-

---

[1] Rosa Ponselle and James A. Drake, *Ponselle: A Singer's Life* (Garden City, NY: Doubleday, 1982) p. 26.

enectady, New York, and married in 1886. Benardino became a saloon-keeper and eventually the proprietor of a boarding house. In 1887, Carmela was born, joined three years later by brother Anthony.

The cold of Schenectady and a typhoid epidemic hastened the young family's move from Schenectady to Waterbury, Connecticut, where Benardino joined his brother Alfonso in the saloon business. Squabbles between Maddelena and Benardino were frequent, and she went to the parish priest for assistance. After Benardino grudgingly accompanied her to the rectory for a conference with the priest, the embarrassed husband felt he could no longer live in Waterbury. He decided the family would move to Meriden, Connecticut. Benardino did well there. In addition to owning and running a saloon, he operated a small farm, bakery, and grocery store. In January of 1897, Rosa Melba Ponzillo was born.[2]

The Ponzillo Sisters

Rosa grew up in the shadow of her older sister Carmela, who was not only beautiful but also had a lovely singing voice. Rosa took piano lessons so she could play as Carmela sang. Rosa then learned to play other instruments as well, all of which she mastered without the benefit of instruction. She loved playing "rag" on piano, such tunes as "The Maple Leaf Rag" and "The Entertainer." In time, Rosa was playing piano for the silent movies at local theaters. Eventually she also sang, as her singing of Italian songs drew many transplanted Italians who sought a little bit of "home."

Meanwhile, Carmela had launched a successful professional career in vaudeville. At the time, vaudeville was much more than the dancers, jugglers, and animal acts as it has come to be known. Much of a typical performance was given over to classical music, giving Carmela the opportunity to sing operatic arias. Eventually she asked Rosa to join her, and the Ponzillo Sisters (also known as "Those Tailored Italian Girls") became an act that was very much in demand. They became headliners on the Keith Circuit, appearing in major theaters, including the Palace in New York, and earning substantial incomes. They made several recordings on the Columbia label.

---

[2]Ponselle and Drake, pp. 1–7.

Destiny Comes into Play

Carmela had been studying in New York and introduced Rosa to her teacher. He liked her voice and arranged a meeting with conductor Romano Romani and Enrico Caruso of the Metropolitan Opera, renowned as the greatest voice in opera. Caruso was impressed and said that, with training, Rosa would some day sing with him at the Met.[3] Caruso wanted to take on the role of Don Alvaro in *La Forza del Destino,* but with the war on, no Italian dramatic sopranos could be brought to the United States, and—until now—there was no one in the states capable of singing that role with the great Caruso. The Met's Managing Director, Giulio Gatti-Casazza, liked Rosa's voice but was reluctant to have a "vaudevillian" singing at the Met. Not only that, Rosa was an American who had never trained in Europe. But her voice won Gatti-Casazza over.

Prior to the debut performance, Gatti-Casazza approached Rosa about changing her name. "Ponzillo," he said, was more difficult to say than "Ponselle," which seemed to have a more international flair. His real reason, however, was to break the association to Carmela and the sisters' vaudeville experience.[4] In addition to gaining a new name, Rosa worked at learning to speak Italian. She had been fluent in her parents' "*Napuletan*" dialect but wanted to master the more formal Tuscan Italian, the language of many of the great Italian composers. Gatti-Casazza gave her a big hug and welcomed her to the Metropolitan as a bona fide *Italiana.*

On November 15, 1918, at the age of 21, Ponselle made her debut at the Metropolitan Opera House in New York as Leonora, opposite Enrico Caruso's Don Alvaro in Verdi's *La Forza del Destino.*[5] Despite her early nervousness—a trait that stayed with her throughout her career—Ponselle did well. "After the final curtain, quite to my surprise, I received almost as many curtain calls as Caruso—a sure sign of my success."[6]

[3] www.rosaponselle.com/news/101696.html
[4] Ponselle and Drake, p. 43.
[5] www.rosaponselle.com/news/101696.html
[6] Ponselle and Drake, p. 55.

Queen of the Met

Ponselle remained at the Met as its reigning queen for 19 seasons, creating new roles and reviving repertoire that had not been attempted by singers for generations. She was considered the greatest Verdian soprano of the twentieth century, and the role in which she established herself as a paradigm to all subsequent generations of singers was Bellini's Norma. This is the role that distinguishes the truly great sopranos from the merely good ones.[7]

Maria Callas, herself a great singer who studied Rosa Ponselle's work, said, "I think we all know Ponselle is simply the greatest singer of us all." Luciano Pavorotti, who also saw Ponselle as a role model, called her the "Queen of Queens of singing."[8]

Opera critic James Huneker called her "The Caruso in petticoats." Diva Geraldine Farrar said that when discussing singers, "There are two you must put aside. One is Enrico Caruso; the other is Rosa Ponselle. Then you may begin to discuss all the others." Leonard Bernstein credited Ponselle with changing the direction of his life when, at eight years old, he heard a recording of her voice.

Outside of the United States, Ponselle sang only at the Royal Opera House at Covent Garden in London (for three seasons) and in Italy (to honor a promise she had made to her mother). She was a great success at both.

Rosa Shocks the World of Opera

In 1937, at age 40, Rosa married Baltimorean Carle A. Jackson. They built a luxurious Mediterranean-style home in Maryland that she called "Villa Pace." At the height of her career and in her vocal prime, Ponselle shocked the world when she retired. Her last performance was in Carmen, April 17, 1937. She continued to sing in concert and to make recordings but she never sang in an opera again. "Her marriage to Jackson was rocky and they divorced in 1949. The breakup was traumatic for Ponselle, and she suffered a nervous breakdown."[9]

---

[7]http://bassocantante.com/opera/ponselle.html
[8]www.rosaponselle.com/news/101696.html
[9]www.rosaponselle.com/news/101696.html

Even in retirement, however, Ponselle maintained the warmth, generosity, sincerity, and humor for which she had been loved by those who knew her. When the Metropolitan staged a "raucous burlesque" called "A Half-Century of Progress," Ponselle sang an aria from *Martha* while riding a bicycle. Bicycling was one of many pastimes that she long enjoyed. Others included mountain climbing and flying airplanes.

Helping the Next Generation of Singers

For the next 44 years of her life, Ponselle devoted herself to giving back. Her pet project was the Baltimore Opera Company. She helped a fundraising drive that enabled the Company to build its own productions. She helped create a Vocal Awards Contest designed to locate promising young talent. For years she sat as a judge in selecting candidates worthy of training assistance and eventual acceptance as performers in the Company's productions. The Company engaged the excellent Baltimore Symphony, and in time the Company became more a professional staff than a group of volunteers, led by Ponselle as Artistic Director.

Ponselle nurtured and launched careers of young operatic talent. Among those she aided who became renowned singers are Beverly Sills, Sherrill Milnes, Placido Domingo, and James Morris. In some instances, she worked with young singers in the studio in her home.

She aided dozens more through the Company. She not only gave more than $3 million to the Company, but she played a very active role in its philosophical, managerial, and artistic decisions. She allowed Villa Pace to be open to the public for three hours a day during "Rosa Ponselle Week" in Baltimore.

In addition, she lent her name to charity events, especially those benefiting children. On a Christmas Day, she spent the afternoon singing carols to the staff and children of New York Nursery and Child's Hospital. On other days, children from Catholic, Protestant, and Jewish orphanages heard an afternoon of classical and popular songs. Between selections, Ponselle spoke about the meanings of words and the lives of composers.

In recognition of her service to the community, Ponselle received an honorary doctoral degree from Our Lady of Notre Dame of Baltimore and the University of Maryland. For having "enhanced the progress and well-being of country and mankind," Rosa was elected to the United States Hall

of Fame Society. Italy awarded her the coveted Order of the Commenda-
tore, making her only the third woman (and first American-born) to have
been so honored.

Rosa Ponselle died on May 25, 1981. On the evening of her funeral in
Baltimore, Luciano Pavarotti was about to give a concert in Tulsa, Okla-
homa. Before he began, he stepped to the stage and said: "Tonight I dedi-
cate my singing to the memory of Rosa Ponselle."[10] A fitting tribute to a
great woman of the opera.

---

[10]Ponselle and Drake, p. 246.

photo: Rosa Ponselle by Herman Mishkin, official photographer of the Metropolitan Opera,
courtesy Dr David S. Shields, University of South Carolina.
http://bassocantante.com/opera/ponselle.html

Renato Turano
Businessman, Senator

In April of 2006, Chicago-area businessman Renato Turano became the first senator to represent the Italian citizens of North and Central America in the Italian Parliament. The magnitude of this event didn't hit home, though, until the freshman representative arrived for his first day on the job.

"When I was a young man, my father always instilled in me that I should maintain my relations with Italy at all times, and especially that I should maintain my ties to the Italian language. By his way of thinking, I might have to return to Italy one day, and I might even have to work there.

"So there I am, walking down the corridors of the Italian Parliament with the guards calling me by name, and my eyes are filling with tears as I think about how proud my father would have been. He was right—I did return to Italy to work—but he never could have imagined in his wildest dreams that I would be returning as a senator.

"Just as that realization was sinking in, the doors to the senate chamber swung open and everybody was yelling, the phones were ringing and it's complete chaos. That's when I knew I had my work cut out for me."

Born to Lead

The eldest of three sons of Mariano and Assunta of Castrolibero, Cosenza, Calabria, Renato Turano was born to lead. His great-grandfather was mayor of Castrolibero in the early 1900s, and his father organized local growers into a cooperative before World War II, vastly improving their bargaining and earning power.

Renato was born in 1942, as war raged across Europe. The economic and physical damages to Calabria were immense, compelling his father to make a fateful decision. "My father came to America three years before I did, but he wasn't happy there. He said he had lost his sense of dignity," Renato says. "In Italy, he had been a coffee salesman who went to work each day dressed in a business suit. In America he had to work in sewer construction. So after 14 months, he told his brother, with whom he was living, that America was not for him."

Once back in Italy, however, Mariano realized he had made a mistake. He may have improved his circumstances, but he knew in his heart that his children would find real opportunity only on the far side of the Atlantic. So he packed his bags once again and moved with his entire family back to the Chicago area in the late 1950s, when Renato was 15.

"My father dreamed of returning to Italy, but he knew that America was the place where his children would have a better future," Renato says. "So, like so many others before him, he left his dream of Italy behind to build a new dream in America."

Mariano went back to working construction during the week, and helped out in his spare time at his brother's business, Carmen Turano Grocery and Bakery. There, he baked bread using an old family recipe. At the time, there was nothing available like his family's hearty four-pound loaf of crusty Italian bread, and he knew his friends and neighbors would enjoy a little taste of the Old Country.

Building a Business

As friendly requests turned into standing bread orders, Mariano focused his attention on growing his business, devising a home-delivery route that he could fulfill in the early morning hours before going to his other job. He finally left the construction business in 1960.

When a fire in 1961 all but destroyed his bakery, Mariano bought an existing business, Campagna Bakery. Over the next few years, he continued to build his client base while his brother Carmen re-opened Turano in partnership with their other brother, Eugene. After Eugene took the helm at Turano, Mariano and Eugene decided to merge their businesses, calling it Campagna-Turano Bakery Inc., the name under which the company is currently incorporated.

"My father and my uncle decided that they would make better partners than competitors," says Renato. "It turned out to be a very wise decision."

After Campagna-Turano opened in Berwyn in 1966, the business quickly transitioned from retail and home delivery to wholesale. The wholesale end of the business skyrocketed, thanks to the company's reputation for quality and the aggressive marketing efforts of brothers Renato, Umberto, and Giancarlo, who eventually bought the business outright.

In 1974, Turano opened a plant in suburban Bloomingdale that produces a full line of cakes, cookies, and pastries. Two years later, the company expanded its Berwyn location to include corporate offices and a 100,000-square-foot production facility that operates seven days a week and produces more than 120 varieties of breads and rolls.

After launching a par-baked line of wholesale goods, Turano expanded again in 1994, this time building a state-of-the-art 100,000-square-foot plant in suburban Bolingbrook. The company opened another plant in Atlanta in 2008, and has plans to open an Orlando facility in 2009. In 1988, *Snack Food and Wholesale Bakery* magazine hailed Turano Baking Co. as Wholesale Baker of the Year.

Today, Renato presides as chairman over one of the largest privately held corporations in the Chicago area. Brother Umberto is president and brother Giancarlo is vice president.

"It's really a leadership of three in one: My brothers and I gather to make decisions together, and we each have our own areas of responsibility," says Renato. "Our company is large, but we run it like a family that includes all of our employees and all of our customers. We don't just sell bread. We build relationships that last a lifetime."

Though running a family business can take a toll on fraternal relations, the brothers Turano haven't lost sight of the fact that they're family, first and foremost.

"As Italians, family is the most important thing," says Renato. "My brothers and I have always been very honest and straightforward with one another. We have a mutual respect, not only as partners but as best friends."

Giving Back

With Renato at the helm, the Turano Baking Co. has established a legendary reputation for generosity.

The Turano Family Foundation makes sizable donations every year to the Greater Chicago Food Depository, research for juvenile diabetes, scholarships for Catholic schools, foundations that extend aid to the inner city and other charities. Beneficiaries within the Italian-American community include the Joint Civic Committee of Italian Americans, Italian Cultural Center, Casa Italia, Columbian Club of Chicago, Italian American Chamber of Commerce-Midwest, Calabresi in America Organization, Italian American Civic Organization of Berwyn, and Società San Francesco di Paola.

Turano has presided over the Columbian Club of Chicago, Calabresi in America Organization, Casa Italia, Italian American Chamber of Commerce-Midwest and Casa Italia.

In recent years, Turano has established himself as an advocate and coalition builder as well as a philanthropist and community leader. He represented the Midwest chamber on the Assocamerestero, an association of 74 Italian chambers of commerce around the world, and he has served since 1994 as *consultore* to the region of Calabria, representing the interests of Calabresi in the United States at annual conferences in Italy.

The University of Wisconsin-Parkside bestowed an honorary doctorate degree on Turano in acknowledgement of an exchange program he started between the University and the University of Calabria. The program enables the schools to exchange students, programs, teachers, seminars, and more.

Turano has also 1) helped the Italian American Chamber of Commerce-Midwest win official recognition from the Italian government; 2) paved the way for the chamber to become a member of Assocamerestero; 3) leveraged funds from the Italian government to support economic exchanges between Italy and the Midwest; 4) brought Calabresi organizations from across North America together for the first time to work for the common good; 5) marshaled resources on both sides of the Atlantic to bring Italian folklore and culture to the Midwest; 6) supported the consul general's Italian language program in Midwest schools.

The city of Berwyn, the state of Illinois, the region of Calabria, and the republic of Italy have all honored Turano for his generosity and dedication, as have the Joint Civic Committee of Italian Americans, Italian Cultural Center, and Italian American Chamber of Commerce.

Senator Turano

In many ways, running for the Italian Senate was the next natural step for Turano.

"I was asked by leaders in America, Canada and Italy to run because they know about my experience and they know that I would be doing this, not for personal gain, but on behalf of Italians living on the continent," he says. "Besides, whenever there's a worthy cause, you can count on me to get involved."

Turano's main mission is to make sure that Italian citizens living abroad have a voice in the affairs of Italian government, and that the Italian government provides its citizens abroad with the services they deserve.

"These are Italians who have made their homes in other countries, but they are Italian citizens nonetheless. Many of them still have property and family in Italy, many of them have needs that the government must meet, and many of them have a valuable perspective that they are willing to share," he says. "They deserve the best that Italy can offer, within the limits of available funds, and they deserve a voice."

His platform includes increasing funding to Italian consulates and improving consular services; eliminating duplication of effort among Italian government offices; increasing funding to Italian programs on the elementary, middle and high school levels, and to Italian organizations that offer Italian courses; increasing cultural programs from Italy and making them more accessible to the community; subsidizing newspapers, radio shows, and television programs that promote Italian image and language; promoting scholastic, cultural, and student exchanges between Italian and American universities; and facilitating trade and other forms of economic exchanges between Italy and North America.

With credentials and a platform that dwarfed his competitors, Turano won the popular vote in the April 2006 elections handily. And as the senatorial candidate for Romano Prodi victorious Partito Democratico, he began the daunting task of representing 460,000 Italian citizens living in North and Central America.

From the moment he stepped off the plane as an Italian senator until the day Romano Prodi's government fell, Renato had only 20 months within which to work, and the prejudice of the entire Parliament to overcome.

"They looked at us as if we were Martians," he recalls. "Their attitude was, 'We know how to run this country. Why are you here?'"

Undaunted, he and the other six senators from abroad formed the Comitato per le Questioni degli Italiani all'Estero, a Senate-approved committee with a dozen Italian counterparts, to address the concerns of their compatriots around the world.

"We were able to legitimize the needs of our constituents as well as the positions that we held," he says. "At the end of the first year, we were able to demonstrate that we had as much to offer them as they had to offer us."

One of the outcomes of this exchange is the impending passage of a law that will restore citizenship to Italians who were forced to relinquish it to become citizens of other countries.

Closer to home, Turano facilitated the creation of a new Italian consulate in New Jersey. He also worked tirelessly to build bridges between universities in America and Italy.

The freshman Italian senator was unseated in his bid for re-election in April of 2008 despite having won the popular vote by a 25-percent margin. The loss came at the hands of an electoral system that favors the success of the party over the success of the individual. Turano bested Basilio Giordano by nearly 3,000 votes, but his Partito Democratico was defeated by Giordano's Partito Popolare Della Libertà, and so Berlusconi and Giordano were in and Veltroni and Turano were out. "It was a tough loss," he says. "But it meant a lot to me that I received the majority (of the popular vote). It says that I had the trust of the Italian citizens living in North and Central America."

Though no longer senator, Turano is still the head of his party (PD) in North and Central America. "We're going to continue to promote these agreements between universities," he says, "and we're going to continue to fight for the rights of Italians living abroad."

---

*Contributors to this profile: Paul Basile, Joe Stella, and Jim Distasio

photo: Paul Basile, *Fra Noi*

VIA FOLIOS

A refereed bok series dedicated to the culture of Italian Americans in North America.

BASSETTI & D'AQUINO, *Italic Lessons*, Vol. 62, Italian/American Studies, $10

GRACE CAVALIERI & SABINA PASCARELLI, EDS., *The Poet's Cookbook*, Vol. 61, Poetry, $12

EMANUEL DI PASQUALE, *Siciliana*, Vol. 60, Poetry, $8

NATALIA COSTA, ED., *Bufalini*, Vol. 59, Poetry, $18

RICHARD VETERE, *Baroque*, Vol. 58, Fiction, $18

LEWIS TURCO, *La Famiglia/The Family*, Vol. 57, Memoir, $15

NICK JAMES MILETI, *The Unscrupulous*, Vol. 56, Humanities, $20

BASSETTI, ACCOLLA, D'AQUINO, *Italici: An Encounter with Piero Bassetti*, Vol. 55, Ital. Studies, $8

GIOSE RIMANELLI, *The Three-legged One*, Vol. 54, Fiction, $15

CHARLES KLOPP, *Bele Antiche Stòrie*, Vol. 53, Criticism, $25

JOSEPH RICAPITO, *Second Wave*, Vol. 52, Poetry, $12

GARY MORMINO, *Italians in Florida*, Vol. 51, History, $15

GIANFRANCO ANGELUCCI, *Federico F.*, Vol. 50, Fiction, $15

ANTHONY VALERIO, *The Little Sailor*, Vol. 49, Memoir, $9

ROSS TALARICO, *The Reptilian Interludes*, Vol. 48, Poetry, $15

RACHEL GUIDO DE VRIES, *Teeny Tiny Tino's Fishing Story*, Vol. 47, Children's Literature, $6

EMANUEL DI PASQUALE, *Writing Anew*, Vol. 46, Poetry, $15

MARIA FAMÀ, *Looking For Cover*, Vol. 45, Poetry, $12

ANTHONY VALERIO, *Toni Cade Bambara's One Sicilian Night*, Vol. 44, Poetry, $10

EMANUEL CARNEVALI, Dennis Barone, Ed., *Furnished Rooms*, Vol. 43, Poetry, $14

BRENT ADKINS, ET AL., EDS., *Shifting Borders, Negotiating Places*, Vol. 42, Proceedings, $18

GEORGE GUIDA, *Low Italian*, Vol. 41, Poetry, $11

GARDAPHÈ, GIORDANO, TAMBURRI, *Introducing Italian Americana*, Vol. 40, ItalAmer.Studies, $10

DANIELA GIOSEFFI, *Blood Autumn/Autunno di sangue*, Vol. 39, Poetry, $15/$25

FRED MISURELLA, *Lies to Live by*, Vol. 38, Stories, $15

STEVEN BELLUSCIO, *Constructing a Bibliography*, Vol. 37, Italian Americana, $15

ANTHONY J. TAMBURRI, ED., *Italian Cultural Studies 2002*, Vol. 36, Essays, $18

BEA TUSIANI, *con amore*, Vol. 35, Memoir, $19

FLAVIA BRIZIO-SKOV, ED., *Reconstructing Societies in the Aftermath of War*, Vol. 34, History, $30

TAMBURRI, ET AL., EDS., *Italian Cultural Studies 2001*, Vol. 33, Essays, $18

ELIZABETH G. MESSINA, ED., *In Our Own Voices*, Vol. 32, Italian American Studies, $25

STANISLAO G. PUGLIESE, *Desperate Inscriptions*, Vol. 31, History, $12

HOSTERT & TAMBURRI, EDS., *Screening Ethnicity*, Vol. 30, Italian American Culture, $25

G. PARATI & B. LAWTON, EDS., *Italian Cultural Studies*, Vol. 29, Essays, $18

HELEN BAROLINI, *More Italian Hours*, Vol. 28, Fiction, $16

FRANCO NASI, ED., *Intorno alla Via Emilia*, Vol. 27, Culture, $16

ARTHUR L. CLEMENTS, *The Book of Madness & Love*, Vol. 26, Poetry, $10

JOHN CASEY, ET AL., *Imagining Humanity*, Vol. 25, Interdisciplinary Studies, $18

ROBERT LIMA, *Sardinia/Sardegna*, Vol. 24, Poetry, $10

DANIELA GIOSEFFI, *Going On*, Vol. 23, Poetry, $10

ROSS TALARICO, *The Journey Home*, Vol. 22, Poetry, $12

EMANUEL DI PASQUALE, *The Silver Lake Love Poems*, Vol. 21, Poetry, $7

JOSEPH TUSIANI, *Ethnicity*, Vol. 20, Poetry, $12

JENNIFER LAGIER, *Second Class Citizen*, Vol. 19, Poetry, $8

FELIX STEFANILE, *The Country of Absence*, Vol. 18, Poetry, $9

PHILIP CANNISTRARO, *Blackshirts*, Vol. 17, History, $12

LUIGI RUSTICHELLI, ED., *Seminario sul racconto*, Vol. 16, Narrative, $10

LEWIS TURCO, *Shaking the Family Tree*, Vol. 15, Memoirs, $9

LUIGI RUSTICHELLI, ED., *Seminario sulla drammaturgia*, Vol. 14, Theater/Essays, $10

FRED GARDAPHÈ, *Moustache Pete is Dead! Long Live Moustache Pete!*, Vol. 13, Oral Lit., $10

JONE GAILLARD CORSI, *Il libretto d'autore, 1860–1930*, Vol. 12, Criticism, $17

HELEN BAROLINI, *Chiaroscuro: Essays of Identity*, Vol. 11, Essays, $15

PICARAZZI & FEINSTEIN, EDS., *An African Harlequin in Milan*, Vol. 10, Theater/Essays, $15

JOSEPH RICAPITO, *Florentine Streets & Other Poems*, Vol. 9, Poetry, $9

FRED MISURELLA, *Short Time*, Vol. 8, Novella, $7

NED CONDINI, *Quartettsatz*, Vol. 7, Poetry, $7

ANTHONY TAMBURRI, ED., *Fuori: Essays by Italian/American Lesbians and Gays*, Vol. 6, Essays, $10

ANTONIO GRAMSCI, P. Verdicchio, Trans. & Intro., *The Southern Question*, Vol. 5, SocCrit., $5

DANIELA GIOSEFFI, *Word Wounds & Water Flowers*, Vol. 4, Poetry, $8

WILEY FEINSTEIN, *Humility's Deceit: Calvino Reading Ariosto Reading Calvino*, Vol. 3, Crit., $10

PAOLO A. GIORDANO, ED., *Joseph Tusiani: Poet, Translator, Humanist*, Vol. 2, Criticism, $25

ROBERT VISCUSI, *Oration Upon the Most Recent Death of Christopher Columbus*, Vol. 1, Poetry, $3

Published by Bordighera, Inc., an independently owned not-for-profit scholarly organization that has no legal affiliation to the University of Florida, the John D. Calandra Italian American Institute, or the State University of New York at Stony Brook.

Breinigsville, PA USA
25 September 2010
246083BV00005B/17/P